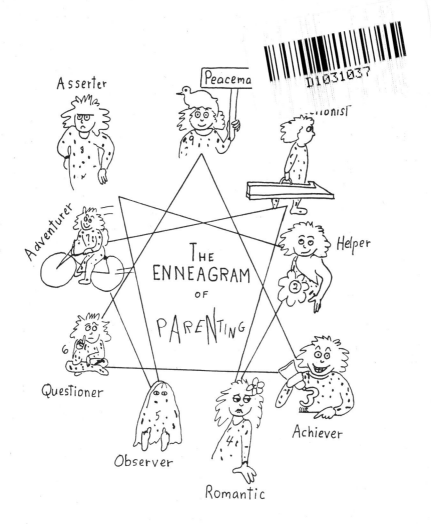

The Enneagram of Parenting

The 9 Types of Children and

How to Raise Them Successfully

Elizabeth Wagele

HarperOne

An Imprint of HarperCollinsPublishers

HarperOne

HarperCollins books may be purchased for educational, business, or sales promotional use. For information please write: Special Markets Department, HarperCollins Publishers, 10 East 53rd Street, New York, NY 10022.

HarperCollins Web site: http://www.harpercollins.com
HarperCollins®, ☰ ®, and HarperOne™
are trademarks of HarperCollins Publishers.

Library of Congress Cataloging-in-Publication Data
Wagele, Elizabeth.
The enneagram of parenting : the 9 types of children and how to
raise them successfully / Elizabeth Wagele.
Includes bibliographical references.
ISBN 978–0–06–251455–4
1. Child psychology.   2. Individual differences in children.   3. Typology (Psychology).   4. Enneagram.
5. Parenting.   6. Child rearing.   I. Title.
HQ772.W13   1997
649'.1—dc20   96–26903

08 09 10 11 12 RRD(H) 20 19 18 17 16 15 14 13

With love to

Gus and our children:

Nick

Martha

Augie, and

Miranda

Contents

Children and the Enneagram

*To be able to help beings, whose needs and
dispositions are so varied, it is necessary to resort
to numerous and diverse methods.*

THE DALAI LAMA

D o you indulge your child or use the drill sergeant's approach? Or do you flail around without a clue as to how to be a parent? If you want to get parenthood off to the best start, or if you want to make a change but don't know how, the wisdom of the Enneagram will help you. People often worry that their kids won't turn out the way they want them to. Since we don't get to choose our kids' personalities, we often try to force them into one. We must learn to adjust to our particular children and encourage them along their own paths.

Before I had children, I thought about what a good mother I'd try to be. I believed that because of my love and dedication my children would be compatible with me in almost every way. At that time, people seemed to think a child's personality unfolded from the parents rather than from inside of the child. Though culture and home environment play important roles in the overall shaping of a person, we have learned that children have an inborn tendency to be either introverted or extroverted, sensitive or insensitive, adventurous or timid, passive or aggressive. They are even born with a tendency toward being either neat or disorganized; it's not just the result of how well their parents trained them.

Adults use the Enneagram for understanding others and for self-growth. The Enneagram also can be applied to children, *if used very carefully*, by helping parents learn how to nurture a sensitive, artistic type, for instance, differently from a rough-and-tumble, conquer-the-world type. Mothers and fathers have been misled or wounded by being told there's one right way to parent and the other ways are wrong.

The Enneagram acknowledges that each of us is unique, yet it identifies certain distinctive patterns of behavior. This intriguing and complex personality system analyzes how we relate to one another according to our differences and similarities. By learning to perceive others more accurately, we will see doors open to greater compassion and acceptance. Parents and teachers learn to

- understand children who are different from them

- appreciate that no type is "better" or "worse" than another

- help children attain a greater sense of confidence and well-being by showing them how to draw on the assets of all nine styles

- show children how to discern and appreciate their own and others' gifts ("David may get better grades on his schoolwork, but you know how to be original. You just have different strengths.")

- ease the minds of those who feel a sense of failure when their child doesn't behave according to their expectations

Children's Nine Styles of Behavior

I grew up in the style of a Five-Observer and was motivated by the drive to know. I needed my family and a few playmates, but I tended to feel less stressed when alone. Most of my friends and classmates had different motivations and styles from mine:

- The One-Perfectionist wanted to get things right.

- The Two-Helper wanted to be liked.

- The Three-Achiever was driven to perform well.

- The Four-Romantic was focused on feelings, concerned with suffering and beauty.

- The Five-Observer was curious and wanted to understand everything.

- The Six-Questioner looked for security.

- The Seven-Adventurer went after newness and fun.

- The Eight-Asserter was strong and energetic.

- The Nine-Peacemaker wanted to be content and to avoid conflict.

Normally, adults see life through the filter of one of these personalities and have trouble understanding the other eight. However, even though children have certain predispositions, they are constantly changing and trying out new ways of behaving. Some of my classmates had taken on a different style or coloring by the time their personalities became fixed in early adulthood. These personalities would in time govern which of *their* children's traits they'd pay attention to or overlook. Among other qualities, for example, *Perfectionist* parents would value goodness and neatness, *Helper* parents would value kindness, *Achiever* parents would value the ability to work well and compete. Hopefully, they learned to perceive and respect their children's special talents and support their interests whether they shared them or not.

History of the Enneagram

The Enneagram (pronounced ANY-a-gram, meaning a figure with nine points) has its roots in the ancient Middle East. It was adapted as a personality typology by Oscar Ichazo and Claudio Naranjo in the 1970s. Information about the types is based on people communicating their experiences to one another. This was first done orally and now is done through writing as well. Interest in the Enneagram has spread rapidly in recent years in the United States and abroad, where it's used as a tool in psychotherapy, in family therapy, in the business world, and for spiritual growth. Focusing on personality differences can benefit society as well as individuals. The Enneagram has great potential for use in schools, for example, by shifting attention away from ethnic, national, and racial differences and toward the personality differences all people share. Classes in the Enneagram are now offered privately and through universities, and one can read books about the Enneagram from varied disciplines on many levels of complexity.

Enneagram Theory

According to the Enneagram, each of us possesses elements of all nine types but in varying degrees. One type is primary, though it might not jell until maturity. We become proficient at viewing the world from one angle, but we can learn to become more flexible and balanced by emulating positive qualities of the other eight types. We begin the continual journey around the Enneagram by focusing on the four types we have the greatest connection to, our "wings" and "arrows."

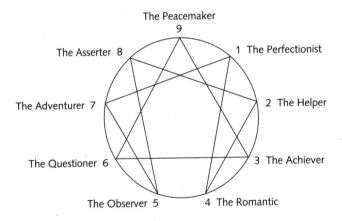

Wings are the neighbors on each side of our Enneagram number.

Arrows are the types at the end of the two lines that radiate out from each number.

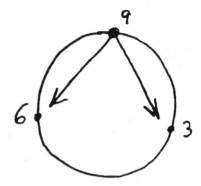

Leaning unconsciously toward our wings and moving along the arrows accounts for many of the variations within each type. For instance, a Four-Romantic who leans more toward her Five-Observer wing may be introverted, while a Four-Romantic who leans more toward her Three-Achiever wing may be extroverted. We can also move intentionally toward our wings and arrows to strengthen certain traits and abilities. This helps to broaden our experience and to be able to respond appropriately to the circumstances we find ourselves in.

By observing our own personality traits, we can learn to understand them as outgrowths of a certain personality type. Stereotyping, however, has dangers: it's possible to respond to someone as though he or she were the label, not the person. The purpose of using the Enneagram with children is just the opposite: to help us experience children's essential selves or spirits by *expanding our awareness* of possible types and traits. We learn to be more accepting of styles different from our own and we learn to constantly remind ourselves that children are far more than all the categories we place them in, including the Enneagram.

Since we need to respect children's natural process of growth and their need to change, I refer to certain outward traits exhibited by kids as Enneagram "styles" in this book rather than as "types." While it's useful for parents and teachers to notice and understand these styles, children's true types can't be determined until they grow up and identify them for themselves.

The Enneagram will become especially alive to you if you figure out your type. Enneagram types in adults are self-identified constellations of internal attitudes, feelings, thoughts, values, and motivations. We can easily be mistaken if we try to guess another's type. For instance, a fearful Six-Questioner may try to camouflage his fear and appear happy-go-lucky (using his Seven-Adventurer wing) or calm (using his Nine-Peacemaker arrow). Therefore, please don't try to assign types to people; only make working hypotheses that you keep to yourself.

About This Book

The ability to parent well depends on accurate observation. The Enneagram helps parents *see* children more in alignment with how the children experience themselves. The first half of each of the nine style chapters is primarily description. The second half of these chapters is called "Approaching Ten Common Problems," and there I present ideas on how to treat the different styles of kids in real-life situations. If you're concerned about a particular problem, such as study habits, I suggest you read the "Study Habits" sections in all nine chapters. In "Twenty Additional Problem Areas," a separate chapter, you will find information about other specific subjects. The Enneagram helps parents open up and ask themselves all kinds of questions about their children and themselves, then accept the answers they find in order to nurture each child in the most appropriate way. If you have serious doubts about something concerning your child or family, I suggest you seek professional help.

Since kids (and adults) don't usually confine their behavior to only one Enneagram style, please read the entire book. Often, two styles share a certain characteristic. I may address it in only one chapter to prevent repetition. Some of my comments pertain to *all* children, not only to children who have the style of a particular chapter. See if you recognize yourself as a child and as a parent in the chapter called "Parents and the Enneagram."

A Word from the Author

The ENNEAGRAM of EMBRYOS

⑨ Can't I just STAY in here? It's so nice and warm.

⑧ I hate being cooped up like this.

① I'm going to sleep all through the night and make my parents happy.

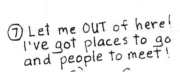

⑦ Let me OUT of here! I've got places to go and people to meet!

② I love Mommy and Daddy SO much. I just can't wait to meet them!

③ Get ready world! Here I come!

⑥ What if they don't like babies? What if my mattress is too hard? What if I don't like their food?

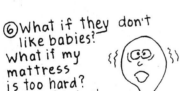

④ I already miss being here.

⑤ What am I doing in here? How can I escape?

The
Perfectionist Style

Hell for a One

Personality Quiz

Does your child

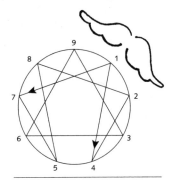

Wings and arrows

○ 1. finish all the food on his or her plate and then gladly help you with the dishes?

○ 2. wash his or her hands and take baths without a fight?

○ 3. do chores without being reminded?

○ 4. have a know-it-all attitude—correct people's grammar, for instance?

○ 5. try to control other children, but not necessarily in a bullying way?

○ 6. tell you better ways to do things and scold you when you're sloppy?

○ 7. have an interest in causes and ideals?

○ 8. take school and homework seriously and criticize those who don't?

If most of your answers are yes, your child is currently behaving in the One style. You can't tell whether a One-ish child will remain this way as an adult.

Perfectionists are usually serious and hardworking. Their wings and arrows can modify this by helping them lighten up and be creative, for example.

If you haven't already, please read the Introduction before proceeding with this chapter.

In order to know how to live "correctly,"
Perfectionists need to be self-critical.

Some One-ish kids *know* there is
only one way to do everything.

A couple of days later . . .

Meanwhile, at another child's house . . .

Some One-ish children try to
keep everyone in line . . .

and some just try to keep
themselves in line.

Karen feels resentful when she makes a mistake.

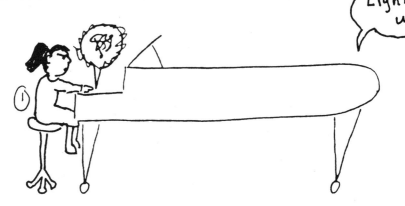

The piano tuna won't quit until he gets it perfect.

Fido taught himself to play the whole piece by ear.

The One style at its healthiest is analytical, balanced, fair, and logical.

Martha had enough patience, perseverance, and foresight to teach her goldfish how to spell. This helped lead Sherlock to the murderer.

One-ish children have an image of an ideal world, which they try to implement by being conscientious, hardworking, and responsible. Since others don't seem to worry as much as they do, they're afraid to show their anxiety and vulnerability. With this pressure on them, they sometimes express anger just below the surface. It's helpful for them to try to lighten up, have fun, and develop the creative side of their personalities.

Approaching Ten Common Problems
with a Child in the Perfectionist Style

Getting to School on Time

Creating order is a never-ending job for Perfectionist-style kids, so they may be late (though rarely) because they had to cross one more thing off their list before they could head out the door. Rather than scolding them for wrongdoing, point out that they might miss something at school if they're tardy. Appeal to the their sense of fairness concerning those they keep waiting, being careful not to make it a guilt trip.

Some One-ish children tend to focus on principles, morals, and ethics, others on being fastidious, neat, and clean. The former think in terms of saving the world in a political or idealistic way and aren't quite as fussy about being on time.

Study Habits

Perfectionist-style kids get stressed out from trying to excel; they tend to worry and get stomachaches and headaches. You're more likely to have problems dealing with their overemphasizing their work than with getting them to study. They need to learn moderation and the skill of pacing themselves. Avoid nagging. One-ish kids are already too hard on themselves.

It's important for ones to engage in activities that are pleasurable and noncompetitive each day, along with their more serious activities.

Manners

Perfectionist-style children can become stressed from worrying about being polite *enough*. They fear exposing their anger and may mistake honesty about their own feelings for rudeness. Create opportunities for self-disclosure, and help them learn to value its importance to their own well-being.

Getting Along with Others

Perfectionist-style children are often very serious and may not feel comfortable with children who are reckless or mischievous. Rather than emphasizing activities that depend on knowledge or skill, encourage noncompetitive ones such as camping out and play-acting.

Plan some idle and fun time each day (this would be unnecessary with an Adventurer child, for instance). If you have teenagers, invite them to do relaxing things with you, such as walking, gardening, and swimming.

Decision Making

Some decisions need to be made subjectively, according to one's whims or feelings, and some objectively, according to the rules or what's sensible. One-ish children excel at the latter. They can place so much importance on doing the "right" thing that they become overly rigid. Encourage them to get in touch with what they really and truly *want* instead of making decisions based solely on what they think they're supposed to want.

When your One-ish children are bent on a decision you disapprove of, offer them choices instead of prescribing one right way. This will teach them which alternatives are okay with you and it will minimize their frustration.

Sleeping and Eating Habits

We spend most of our lives sleeping and eating, so it's important that these two activities be as stress-free as possible. It seems unfair to order children to bed with the lights off before they can possibly sleep, for example. Either let them stay up with the family a little later or play quietly in their room or bed until they fall asleep. Don't insist that they eat things they hate. A simple sandwich or cereal can be substituted. Taking a reasonable attitude of compromise (they can't eat potato chips for breakfast but they don't *have* to eat eggs) won't produce a spoiled child.

Try to keep meals pleasant by gently encouraging family members to listen to one another and to speak one at a time. Don't make this a hard-and-fast rule; if only the adults do it, it's a good start. One-ish kids usually want to learn good manners, but if one of your children misbehaves, have her sit up close to or touching an adult, or send her to another room to eat alone. Be present for your children; I used to feel neglected when my father read the newspaper at the table. Emphasize meals as a time to be together and to enjoy one another's company more than as an opportunity to teach perfect manners.

Standing Up for Himself or Herself

Perfectionist-style children are strong-minded, have a well-developed sense of justice and ethics, and are not easily pushed around. They may go too far, however, and hang onto their positions too rigidly. Ask them to think about what a person with the opposite point of view might experience.

Get-Up-and-Go

One-ish children usually have a lot of energy and are motivated to develop their skills and get the job done.

Practice makes perfect. Kailen was soon able to shoot down his own meals.

Emotional Maturity

Children acting in the style of a Perfectionist can lock themselves into an analytical attitude that leaves little room for creative or feeling sides of their personalities. Expose them to classes in the arts, such as dance, finger painting, drumming—the more free-form the better for loosening them up. Take One-ish children to a wide range of movies, and watch cartoons and comedy shows with them. Show them that it's okay, even necessary, to make mistakes. If you are a One parent, this may be hard for you.

Responsibility

Be careful not to become too dependent on your One-ish child's goodness or helpfulness; it will deprive him or her of the chance to frolic and be a kid.

Parents are tempted to pressure One-ish children because the results make them feel they did a good job of parenting. Perfectionist-style kids find fault with themselves all too easily and need to be treated with positive regard to bolster their self-esteem. Encourage them to be playful and silly and to do things they really enjoy. Introduce them to fairy tales and to worlds of the imperfect, such as the Fool and the Witch. Gracefully admit mistakes, failures, and being wrong. If you accept these experiences in yourself, it will relieve the pressure on your child.

At the age of ten, Ann liked to write down license numbers as neighbors' cars passed in front of her house.

The
Helper Style

Personality Quiz

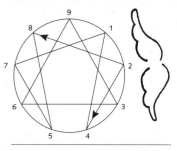

Wings and arrows

Does your child

○ 1. often put other people's desires first and rarely ask for what he or she needs?

○ 2. get his or her feelings hurt easily?

○ 3. have an attraction to those with problems and enjoy giving them advice?

○ 4. know how to get people to do what he or she wants by helping or complimenting them?

○ 5. like to be with other people more than almost anything?

○ 6. get attention by pleasing or showing off?

○ 7. try to be good at school?

○ 8. seem to know what people want or need without being told?

If most of your answers are yes, your child is currently behaving in the Helper style. This child may or may not remain this way as an adult.

I related strongly to the Two style when I was a child – especially the part about rescuing baby animals.

If you haven't already, please read the Introduction before proceeding with this chapter.

Two-ish children like to
do things for others.

They can be
very kind . . .

and help
those in
need.

Two-ish creatures have a great fondness for people.

They support and protect their loved ones.

Helper-style children feel betrayed and rejected when they have problems with people.

Two-ish children try to
receive love and approval by

performing
well,

giving
good
advice,

helping people
feel comfortable,

and
being
cute.

Sometimes they like *not* thinking about people for a change.

They get tired of acting nice and trying to tell people what they want to hear.

Pleasing others takes energy that could be put into expanding themselves and finding out who *they* are. They can feel more balanced when they're able to

be alone with their own thoughts,

pursue creative activities,

and be more assertive and direct.

Give me a couple of trout - on the double.

Approaching Ten Common Problems
with a Child in the Helper Style

Getting to School on Time

Helper-style children generally want to be good and get to school on time. For many, though, the drama of dealing with a homeless kitten found on the way will take precedence. Hopefully, their teacher will see the virtue in this if it doesn't happen too often.

Only YOU can save me!

Study Habits

Two-ish children, more than others, may want to continue interacting with their classmates when school lets out instead of buckling down to homework. If possible, have them start their homework right after school, and reward them with free time later. If separation from their friends is too wrenching, either have them do their homework together or schedule it regularly for later in the day. Since Two-ish children are sensitive and want to please, give them consistency and structure and try not to treat them in a heavy-handed way.

Manners

Most children in the Helper style are well behaved and polite—superficially at least. For those who are excitable and attention seeking, think of constructive outlets for their energy and have projects ready for when riding in the car, on the bus, and so on. Enforce certain rules, such as no grabbing at others' belongings and no hitting, but otherwise teach them manners little by little. In some Two-ish children, disobedience could be a positive sign that they're willing to risk disapproval.

Two-style children may hide or deny their hostile feelings, even while expressing them. If someone suggests Two-ish children have angry motivations, they either may have no idea what the person is talking about or may become devastated. Let them know over a period of time that moderate anger is acceptable to you, both from them and from people in general. Tell them it's okay to be angry.

Sleeping and Eating Habits

With all children, avoid serious conflicts over sleeping and eating. If they have problems with sleeping or if they experience night terrors, hold and comfort them. If they're fussy eaters, trust this to improve with age. Don't interfere by criticizing, hovering over them, or putting them on diets. If problems persist, seek professional help.

Troubled or fearful children sometimes soothe themselves with food or excess sleep. Try to find out if your child feels worried, embarrassed, or sad about something. If discussing feelings bothers you, talk about it with a friend or therapist.

Getting Along with Others

Some Two-ish kids are socially adept.

However, they may have a tendency to be manipulative, overly controlling, or bossy.

When they're direct and treat others fairly, be sure to praise them. If they uncharacteristically shy away from other children, look for possible reasons and talk to them about it. Take charge and invite classmates over to have a party, draw, or play games. Try to teach them they don't need approval from *everyone*.

Standing Up for Himself or Herself

Most Helper-style children are extroverted and want to be seen in a good light. Take their opinions seriously and express your confidence in them in order to help them become more self-reliant and assertive. Some give in too easily, but others are spunky and can be extremely persuasive.

Decision Making

Two-ish children are often out of touch with their real desires: they may wait and see what everyone else is going to do, or they may do what they think will make others like them. Help them connect with themselves by asking which tastes, colors, and smells they prefer. Art and Rebecca play a game where all the members of the family present and defend their opinions about a chosen subject. It can be about current events, movies they've seen together, or something silly. Playing this regularly has helped their Two-ish child, Marge, with her decision-making abilities, her individuality, and her confidence.

Get-Up-and-Go

Wanting to be with other children usually motivates Two-ish children. See if you can encourage enthusiasm for nonsocial as well as social activities. Take Two-ish children to visit some workplaces: yours or your friends'. Go for a walk in the woods or on the beach just to be together in nature without talking. Enroll them in interesting classes, and take them to a large variety of museums, aquariums, and other sights.

Emotional Maturity

Two-ish children live in the world of relationships and feelings. It's very important to them to be liked. Balance their focus on people by telling them about the world and how things work. If you don't accept their emotionality, they may feel you don't love them, so listen to their hurts and take their feelings seriously.

They need a large base of support; if they receive sufficient approval at home, they won't need to seek it in unhealthy ways. Try to see conflicts their way, and encourage them to be direct.

Unlike Nine-Peacemakers, who see things from all angles and are natural mediators, Two-Helpers tend to zero in on one person at a time. They can adapt their own personality to fit the person they're with. Trying to relate to several at the same time can be confusing and stressful for them. Therefore, arrange for them to have time alone with each parent regularly.

To help Two-ish kids gain a healthy perspective on reality, enrich their environment and let them learn from experience. These kids fall into denial easily and can see situations as perfect when they aren't. It's okay to point out the other side to them and encourage them to see what they may have been denying, if you do it gently. If your child frequently becomes furious, enraged, or hysterical, seek outside help.

Responsibility

Helper-style children get practice being responsible by doing what they love to do: taking care of pets, soothing friends, and trying to help people solve problems.

They can read people well, and they may use this ability either for great good or to get their way. Steer them away from manipulating others by being direct yourself; let Betty know you are letting her to go to Penny's house to wrap gifts because you really like the idea, *not* just because she charmed you into it.

Some styles of children, especially Twos and Threes, are more focused on what others think about them (their image) than with what they think or feel themselves. If your child is a Two and you're not, try to accept your differences, and be ready to help your child develop his or her own values and individuality.

The Enneagram of Blankies

The
Achiever

Personality Quiz

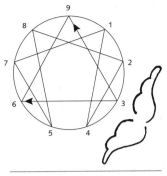

Does your child

    ○ 1. persevere to get things accomplished?

    ○ 2. often become the teacher's pet?

    ○ 3. fit well into the social scene?

    ○ 4. like to be clean, polished, and well dressed?

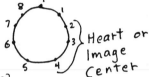

Wings and arrows

    ○ 5. have a great deal of energy yet become overly tired from too much doing?

    ○ 6. have many abilities and interests?

    ○ 7. have a quick and efficient mind?

Heart or Image Center

    ○ 8. seem optimistic and confident most of the time?

If most of your answers are yes, your child is currently behaving in the Achiever style. There's no way to tell if a Three-ish child will remain this way as an adult.

BRAVO!

If you haven't done so already, please read the Introduction before proceeding with this chapter.

Three-ish children
are always busy
and active.

They owe their
accomplishments
to being practical
and persistent.

They love it
when people
feel proud
of them.

They have
the ability
to inspire,
coach, and
talk people
into things.

Three-ish children set
high goals for themselves.

Many place great
importance on
looking really,
really good . . .

and having friends
who look good . . .

Get a shell if you
want to crawl around
with me, Sluggo. I have
a thing about image.

so they keep track of what's in style.

Do you like traveling in a piece of junk?

Achiever-style kids see opportunities everywhere. Failure isn't even an option.

I know I'll make it 'cause I've been training at the gym!

Help!

Help!

If Freddy does fail, he'll somehow find a way to turn it into an opportunity.

Achiever-style children become stressed from working, competing, and being "on." Encourage them to view relaxing (which they see as laziness) as a task that's necessary for their well-being.

Let them know they're loved and lovable for who they are, without having to earn praise. Devote time to nurturing their feelings, and encourage them to develop meaningful friendships.

The core issue for Threes is honesty. The problem is that they don't claim what's theirs—their own personal world of feelings and priorities. Instead, their image becomes all-important. Parents can help Three-ish children balance this tendency to impress the outer world by showing respect for their inner life, by helping them to discover what they truly care about, and by encouraging them to develop their own principles.

Approaching Ten Common Problems
with a Child in the Achiever Style

Getting to School on Time

Achiever-style children are usually positively involved in school and want to be on time. If they have problems with tardiness, check into how they're getting along with their teacher and with the other students. This may take perseverance on your part, as they aren't always forthcoming about difficulties they're having.

Make mornings easier by having them set the table and do other jobs the night before. Starting around junior high school, they may need to get up earlier for last-minute studying or primping.

Study Habits

Achiever-style children want to excel, but they may take shortcuts or bite off more than they can chew. Their clear thinking and organizing skills equip

them well for schoolwork. They want to be liked and seen as special by their teachers, but occasionally they get into trouble from behaving arrogantly or assertively.

Ali packed two lunches for herself every day in high school, one for noon and one for dinner, since her activities lasted until late into the evening. When Grace decided to go to college in the sixth grade, it was a foregone conclusion that she'd get a Ph.D.—and she did.

Manners

Achiever-style kids usually absorb good manners because they want to make a good impression. When Marc went to his first high school athletics awards dinner, he worried about how to keep the chicken and spinach from clinging to his teeth and the spaghetti sauce off his well-scrubbed face and white shirt.

COME TO The Three Club's SUCCESS CLASSES ✻ ✻ After school Mondays Subjects include:
• Advanced Shmooze
• Silent Burping
• Latest Fashions
• and much more...

Getting Along with Others

Achiever-style kids are usually popular leaders. They believe others should—or want—to be like them, and they have difficulty understanding those who aren't. If they're not accepted easily, they may be too devastated to persist openly. They often have many acquaintances. Encourage them to value and cultivate close friendships as well.

Especially if you're an introverted parent of a Three-ish child, remember that they are motivated by keeping active and going after results. When anything stands in the way of this, they may become irritable. Try not to diminish their accomplishments or be put off by their need to perform for approval. Appreciate how strongly the children *feel* about their accomplishments—more than the accomplishments themselves.

Sleeping and Eating Habits

Achiever-style children have energy to burn, so they may not want to go to sleep when it's bedtime. Set up a routine of reading them quiet stories to help them wind down for the night.

These children want to be healthy and fit and are usually motivated to eat what's good for them. Try especially to make mealtimes calm so the Three-ish child can enjoy the family being together. Eating and sleeping should be as pleasurable and free from stress as possible; ask yourself if you're too strict or if you're not structured enough. If you have serious worries about your child's eating habits, seek professional help. You might first read the section on eating disorders in "Twenty Additional Problem Areas."

Standing Up for Himself or Herself

Three-ish children usually excel at using their verbal and social skills for self-promotion and self-presentation. Some bend over backward to please everyone else and need to be reminded to please themselves with their efforts. When they don't get their way, they sometimes speak louder and louder until they're noticed.

Decision Making

Three-ish children don't like to waste time and are usually very decisive and self-reliant. They like to take care of business and get on to the next thing.

Get-Up-and-Go

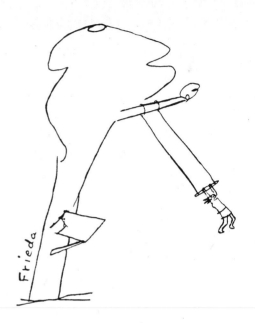

*You can't keep a squirrel
on the ground—especially
in timbered country.*

FRED ADDISON
Heavener, Oklahoma

Some parents may see their Three-ish children as *too* energetic, determined, and motivated. Parents need to encourage their children to relax and unwind if they become stressed. Have some activities available for them to do that are repetitive, mellow, and noncompetitive.

Emotional Maturity

Achiever-style children identify with the crowd and the culture and can be overly influenced by others. Help them come back to themselves by regularly asking questions about their personal values, such as, "What do *you* like? Which is *your* favorite?" Encourage creativity, working for a cause, and helping people out. If you are a Three parent, try not to brag about your child and show him or her off. This will reinforce rather than balance the child's Three-ness. Give attention to Three-ish children's inner feelings. Experience their inner being.

Responsibility

Three-ish children are usually responsible about meeting their own goals but are sometimes too absorbed in their lives to meet other obligations. Parents can help by emphasizing the importance of loyalty and looking out for one another. Assign these kids tasks like taking care of pets.

If you're not very organized, try to adapt to your Three-ish children by helping their lives run more smoothly and effectively.

The
Romantic Style

Personality Quiz

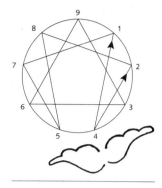

Does your child

○ 1. have feelings that are easily hurt?

○ 2. want to be seen as special?

○ 3. have, or want to have, a closet full of dress-up clothes?

○ 4. soul-search and/or engage in fantasy play?

○ 5. have a sense of the dramatic—both tragic and comic?

○ 6. enjoy the arts or collect beautiful treasures?

○ 7. look at things in a special, creative way?

○ 8. seem depressed or melancholy at times?

Wings and arrows

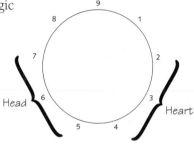

Head center meets heart center.

If most of your answers are yes, your child is currently behaving in the Romantic style. He or she may relate primarily to another style as an adult.

I resonate strongly with my Four wing. Even though it's not good to "type" other people, some people have decided (wrongly) that I was a Four.

If you haven't already, please read the Introduction before proceeding with this chapter.

Romantic-style children find everyday life boring and tedious.

④

They prefer the excitement of participating in or experiencing the theater, dance, art, and music. They also enjoy movies, the purity and loveliness of beautiful objects, what they can do with their own imagination, and that which is enchanting, mysterious, and unpredictable.

Here is a poem written by a musical and artistic child; it is entitled "The Furry Goose."

Furry Goose	Furry Geese
Furry Moose	Furry Meese
Furry Lice	Für Elise

Even though Four-ish children are often friendly and warm, they sometimes feel shy and lonely . . .

are overpowered by their own emotions . . .

or wonder if they belong.

Pet Show

Sometimes Romantics want whatever they *don't* have . . .

and sometimes they want what someone *else* has.

Sometimes they think others want what *they* have.

Just as cats

give special

meaning to

certain places . . .

these children

find special

meaning where

others may not.

Four-ish children have especially delicate feelings and can fill with shame when people are angry with them.

They long to have a deep heart connection with a soul mate.

Four-ish children often feel misunderstood, so it's important to listen carefully to them. You don't have to get caught up in their feelings if they're very intense, just acknowledge what they are feeling. Sometimes it's helpful for these children to get out of their internal world, join in with others, and contribute their cleverness and sense of humor.

Approaching Ten Common Problems with a Child in the Romantic Style

Getting to School on Time

The more introverted Four-ish children are shy, have trouble being around people for long periods of time, and find grammar school frightening. Those who are extroverted (there are probably fewer of these) are outgoing and look forward to pleasing their teachers and seeing other children. Emotions can control Romantic-style kids. A four-year-old I know was counting on marrying his nursery school friend when they grew up. When her family moved a few miles away, he was inconsolable and wailed all night long. Needless to say, he arrived late to school the next day.

A misplaced shoe in the morning can throw Four-ish children into hysteria or paralysis, so take the precaution of laying out their clothes (if they're very young) and making sure their homework is located the night before. Four-ish kids will also be slowed down by feeling left out, by a fight with a friend, or by a low-level depression. Monday mornings are usually the most difficult for children who have trouble with transitions. This is when stomachaches are most likely to occur. If your child has this problem, you might suggest that he or she call you from school later in the morning to ease the stress.

Study Habits

If Romantic-style children have trouble starting their homework, explore the reason for it. Plan plenty of time for studying in case they have hurt feelings that need soothing or a bad mood interferes.

Are there family problems or difficulties at school? Develop good communication so Four-ish children feel comfortable telling you what's bothering them. Since they express their feelings in many ways, not only verbally, it's important to learn to read them.

School can be a good outlet for Romantic-style creativity through plays, bands, orchestras, art classes, and creative writing. Howard, for example, always presented his reports in rhyme.

Manners

Romantic-style children are often compliant and don't want to offend. If they aren't appreciated, however, they can feel resentful and become aggressive or say biting things. Let them know what manners you expect. However, if someone violates one of their strongly held principles, Four-ish kids will be unable to hide their feelings. See this as a strength, and help them find appropriate ways to express their differences.

Getting Along with Others

Romantic-style children tend to have strong likes and dislikes with regard to other people. They long to have a special soul mate with whom to share their inner world. While they can be very warm and giving to close friends, their envy can get the better of them and they may become hostile. For example, David was always sure that his friends' vacations were far better than his own.

If your Four-ish kid is withdrawn, don't plunge him or her abruptly into new social situations. Suzie hated going to visit people she wasn't familiar with and would stay in her parents' car to avoid facing them. John, though, was okay as long as his parents stayed with him while he overcame his initial fear. Remember, introverted children need to limit the amount of time they spend with others, and they need your understanding in this. Don't expect them to be able to spend a day at school, then go to a scout meeting, and *then* go home with a friend.

Danny hates rough play, but he loves romantic stories about heroes. He and his active cousin, Ethan, used to have trouble finding a way to play together. One day Ethan began acting out Danny's tales of knights by galloping around, sword-fighting, and slaying dragons. Now they're never at a loss for what to do.

Sleeping and Eating Habits

Emotional reactions can interfere with Four-ish (and all children's) sleep and eating.

See if you can talk things out with them. When they're young, though, they sometimes don't know what they feel. Chat with them about events of the day, and mention some of your own feelings that might touch upon theirs. Rituals such as bedtime stories can mean a lot to them.

It's important for these children to feel calm and secure concerning sleeping and eating. Swallowing becomes difficult if family tension is served along with the food. Explain family situations in such a way that children realize the problems are not their fault. Find out from observing them how much structure they're comfortable with.

You'd better go to bed if you're too sleepy to listen, mom.

Standing Up for Himself or Herself

Romantic-style children have high principles and often want to save the world. The more outgoing of them engage in competition and like to argue their deeply held convictions. Some are shy, however, and cave in, shut down, or sidle away to a private place. Help strengthen their confidence and self-esteem. Stand up for them if they can't do it themselves, decreasing your protection over time.

Decision Making

Romantic-style children usually have strong values and know what they like. When they forget themselves, however, it may be because they're trying to please someone else. For the most part, they value and can rely on what their feelings or gut reactions tell them.

WOW!

Get-Up-and-Go

Though Four-ish children can be languid or brooding, they are usually able to muster up energy when a principle is at stake, when a close friend needs them, or when they have an idea for an exciting creative project. Some will put themselves in a scary situation just to stimulate their adrenaline and feel more alive, though many are too fearful to do this.

Emotional Maturity

Romantic-style children are very sensitive to pressure by a parent to be a certain way (to be just like the parent, usually). Find the subtleties and complexities in their personalities. Honor the differences between the two of you in order to help your Four-ish child build a sense of self.

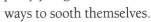

If you feel threatened by Four-ish kids' ferocious feelings, try to understand their need to engage emotionally. Try to stay present and be a good listener. They'll appreciate your seeing them through rough times. Be honest and tell them if intense exchanges upset you.

Four-ish children fear abandonment. They can be jealous, self-critical, and self-punishing. Set up activities where they'll feel successful, and show them you truly love and perceive them. They will internalize the attention and sympathy you give them and learn ways to sooth themselves.

The Unfinished Sympathy

I have to make dinner, but we'll talk about this later— OK?

OK, mom.

Idea contributed by Rebecca Mayeno.

As they enter their teens, help them question the validity of any pessimistic or hopeless thoughts they may have about themselves. The most important thing, though, is to listen to them in a way that lets them know you understand what they're telling you. If they seem extremely depressed or suicidal, get professional help.

Responsibility

Four-ish children, like their One-Perfectionist arrow, can be very conscientious. They're humanitarian and will step in to protect a mistreated child or animal. Encourage friendships with elderly people in the neighborhood who may welcome their attention. Outlets for their compassion and altruism also include help-

ing out at a hospital or senior center and raising guide dogs for the blind.

If responsibility slackens, Four-ish children may be suffering over something or going through a rebellious cycle. Be available to listen to their problems. Adult Fours sometimes say that as a child, without knowing why, they felt sad and lonely.

The purpose of art is that it teaches us things about ourselves that we would not know otherwise.
PIANIST BILL EVANS

To soul-searching Romantic-style teens, the meaning of life is something that cannot be defined but only felt. They may not like systems, such as the Enneagram, that try to pin them down. Melancholy, which also can't be defined in words, connects them to the mysteries of the universe. If anyone could add to their life, some Fours believe, it would be only a great artist or a great love.

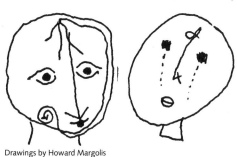

Drawings by Howard Margolis

Parents and teachers sometimes don't understand that introversion is restorative and crucial to a Four-ish child's creative process. They may misinterpret soul searching and dreaming as unproductive. I admire Romantic-style children for not being afraid to express their emotions, including the joyous *and* the sad.

The Enneagram of Nosebleeds

The
Observer Style

Personality Quiz

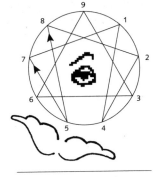

Wings and arrows

Does your child

○ 1. have a quiet or shy personality?

○ 2. like to be alone—get lost in reading or other interests?

○ 3. have definite opinions about most things but show willingness to listen to other interpretations?

○ 4. have an interest in how things work or in philosophical questions?

○ 5. have a whimsical sense of humor?

○ 6. tend to stay separate or hover around the edge of groups?

○ 7. seem uninterested in social norms?

○ 8. dislike it when people pry or lavish too much attention on him or her?

If most of your answers are yes, your child is currently behaving in the Five style. This doesn't necessarily represent a permanent type.

I like to watch.

If you haven't already, please read the Introduction before proceeding with this chapter.

Five-ish children are curious
and have active minds.

They have no
problem
entertaining
themselves.

1.

Parents often have trouble understanding that Five-ish children can be happy when alone, and they may prod their kids to do things they don't want to do.

This child thought his parents were too invasive. He tried to get them to let up by whispering subliminal propaganda.

Five-ish children frighten easily, especially when they see people fighting with each other or when they're put on the spot.

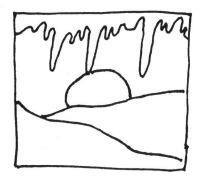

Since they watch and
observe more than
most children . . .

they may
see things
that others
don't see.

A Five I once
knew was so
quiet, he

Felt out of place in society.

His knees,
they would knock

When he tried
to small-talk

But his theories brought
much notoriety.

Five-ish children don't usually care about social conventions and don't always interact easily. They may feel awkward or different from other children. Never push them, but gently invite them to join in.

Loud or unpleasant sounds offend Five-ish children's sensitive nervous systems. When noise is forced on them, they may take it as another form of someone trying to control them. They'll do almost anything to avoid unpleasantness. Some wish they could speak without thinking about it so much first. One-to-one contact is often more comfortable than being in groups.

Approaching Ten Common Problems with a Child in the Observer Style

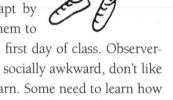

Getting to School on Time

Observer-style children will usually get to school on time rather than risk being stared at as they walk in late. Some will do almost anything to stay unobserved.

Study Habits

Changes, such as starting kindergarten, can be terrifying for Five-ish children. They worry that their teachers will make impossible demands. Try to help them adapt by walking them leisurely through the school. Introduce them to their teacher, principal, and a few classmates before the first day of class. Observer-style teens may hold back from school because they feel socially awkward, don't like competing, or aren't getting taught what they want to learn. Some need to learn how *not* to study so much and may profit from becoming involved in outside activities.

Our culture used to be especially difficult for certain Fives who were nerdy "eggheads." They didn't fit the ideals of the well-dressed charmer or the rugged outdoorsman, and they tended to talk about scientific things nobody but other nerds could understand. Since the coming of personal computers, however, Fives have more status. Bill Gates, the chair of Microsoft Corporation and the richest man in America, is a Five who's really made it. An entrepreneurial and technical genius, he rides buses and doesn't impose a dress code on his employees.

Observer-style children have strong consciences and want to do things according to their own principles. They don't like it when others try to caretake or intrude into their business, so they have a built-in difficulty with Two-Helper mothers, fathers, and teachers. If you're a Two, try meeting Five-ish children with whimsical humor at your Four arrow and at their Four wing. If they have a stronger Six wing, they may live more in their heads, their humor might be sarcastic, and the differences between you may be more difficult to surmount. Whatever your type, if you need to remind them to study, be brief and objective.

Manners

Most Five-ish children don't want to make waves, but they do want to know reasons for traditions instead of following them blindly. "Just because it's done" doesn't hold water for them.

Sometimes Five-ish children keep to themselves at family reunions. If Aunt Tillie doesn't understand why Jaki spends most of the Thanksgiving gathering reading instead of conversing for three hours, let Tillie know this is just Jaki's style.

Getting Along with Others

As the name suggests, Observer-style kids tend to stay on the sidelines. When they do join in, they're often surprised to find that *doing* feels so different from *watching*. Because of the cultural bias toward extroversion, it is especially important to show confidence in your introverted kid, as most Five-ish children are. You can make a big difference in this area of your child's life by being perceptive and sensitive.

Extroverted parents can feel like failures for not instilling the enjoyment of social life in their Five-ish kids. These children aren't likely to have a million friends or to love going to parties.

The Mediterranean Flute Fry.

Sanskrit

Even introverts need at least one good pal to connect with.

Let your children know you like their company, but show understanding by not insisting upon it. Help them be less fearful by exposing them to compatible people. Rather than signing them up for purely social activities, sign them up for small classes in subjects they're truly interested in.

Most Observer-style kids can't pretend they have something in common with people when they don't. Parents should view this aspect of Five-ishness—of not being compelled to compete, impress, or be on stage for other people—as a strength.

Sleeping and Eating Habits

Five-ish kids love their privacy. Staying up into the late hours, when they don't have to worry about people distracting or bothering them, can give them a magical feeling of freedom. As head center–style kids, they are especially subject to fears, fretting, and phobias and often have sensitive nervous systems.

If they or other styles of children want more independence around meals, stock the kitchen with nutritious food to nibble on, and teach them how to prepare some tasty things for lunch and snacks. At least one meal a day (dinner) should be enjoyed together with the whole family. Try to keep eating and sleeping as free from conflict as possible.

Standing Up for Himself or Herself

Some Five-ish children defend themselves well verbally and will argue about almost anything. Others accommodate in order to avoid discord and may merge with the woodwork or slither out of the room when unhappy or upset. Observer-style children need to feel safe and supported. They don't trust overpowering people.

Trevor's sense of fairness inspired him to really stand up to his father one day. He and a friend were throwing dirt clods against the garage door in a game of skill. His father came out, told them to stop, and explained that they were renting the house and mustn't get it dirty. Trevor completely understood the situation, and for him the matter was resolved. Then his father did a completely unnecessary thing and *spanked* him! The incensed child delivered a scathing speech to his errant father, and that spanking turned out to be Trevor's last.

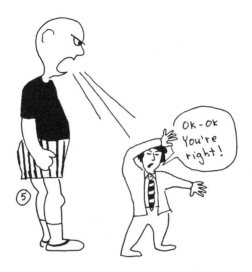

Decision Making

My life is as simple as I can make it. Work all day, then cook, eat, wash up, telephone, hack writing, drink, and television in the evenings. I almost never go out. I suppose everyone tries to ignore the passing of time: some people by doing a lot, being in California one year and Japan the next; or there's my way—making every day and every year exactly the same. Probably neither works.

PHILIP LARKIN, A FIVE

Observer-style kids form lots of opinions, but, being introverted, they don't think as fast on their feet as many others do. Decisions, such as what to order at a restaurant, can be difficult for them. When I was a child, I always wanted to try something new and delicious, but I never had enough time. I'd panic when the waiter arrived for my order, and I'd take fried chicken—again. Many Five-ish children, however, take comfort in *knowing* they'll choose the same thing every time.

Give your children practice in making decisions by taking them out at least twice a day to choose a triple ice cream cone (just kidding).

Get-Up-and-Go

Observer-style children are curious and motivated to learn, but they don't usually broadcast their accomplishments. Accept their introverted style and their lack of interest in high-profile activities, such as running for school office.

Emotional Maturity

For Observer-style children, anger and negativism can go underground and get stuck there. Gently encourage "doing" for balance: scouting, painting, music, sports, or dancing—especially activities that are physical and spontaneous. Help Five-ish children get in touch with their feelings by being an attentive listener. Be careful not to intrude or to give advice. However, you can help break their self-isolation by validating and mirroring their opinions. Being onlookers, they feel separate and different from others and often believe something's wrong with them. Some imagine (or hope) that as long as they hold still they won't be noticed. By saying, "You observe well—your interpretations are valuable to us," parents can show their children that they're a part of the picture, they belong, and they're appreciated.

Responsibility

Observer-style children usually have the conscience, sense of fairness, and self-discipline to be responsible. Plan their chores with them, or tell them what you want and give them a time frame. If they don't do their jobs, be more firm but don't lecture or browbeat.

Introverted Five-ish kids are often a mystery to extroverted (and some introverted) parents. They often feel an underlying hurt, anger, and alienation because their parents', school's, and society's values and realities are given more legitimacy than their own. They may reinforce their isolation by convincing themselves they don't need anyone.

One way to understand your Five-ish children is by making the effort to join in on their sense of humor and to learn to laugh with them. Also, develop an interest in the music, movies, and writers they like. Take a genuine interest in ther world, rather than trying to manipulate them into a relationship.

The
Questioner Style

Personality Quiz

Does your child

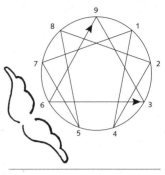

Wings and arrows

1. worry about safety more than most kids?
2. react in extreme, contradictory, or unpredictable ways at times?
3. change moods often: nervous, brooding, enraged, comical, serious?
4. like to argue the opposite side from everybody else?
5. act insecure, suspicious, and frightened? Or cover these feelings by being overly aggressive?
6. try to entertain or please and get people to like him or her?
7. talk fast or in a stuttering kind of way?
8. have compassion for people who suffer?

If most of your answers are yes, your child is currently behaving in the Six style. This doesn't necessarily predict his or her adult Enneagram type.

My Six wing is the center of my FEAR or HEAD center.

If you haven't already, please read the Introduction before proceeding with this chapter.

The three centers

Questioner-style children can seem either shy and fearful or aggressive and fearless. They all want to feel more secure.

This piano likes having someone take care of him.

They try to be loyal to themselves and to others.

JOIN OUR CAUSE

RAISE YOUR DAUGHTER'S ALLOWANCE

I NEED MORE

BE FAIR

BE GENER-OUS

These Six-ish kids like to resolve conflicts and band together for a good cause.

It's important to try to figure things out. However, Six-ish kids often get stuck in the thinking and worrying process and don't come to a conclusion. They're usually on the alert for danger and may panic over little things.

Questioner-style children can also be brave, strong, quick tempered, rebellious, and antiauthoritarian.

They can
worry about
everything . . .

which can
lead to taking
extra precautions.

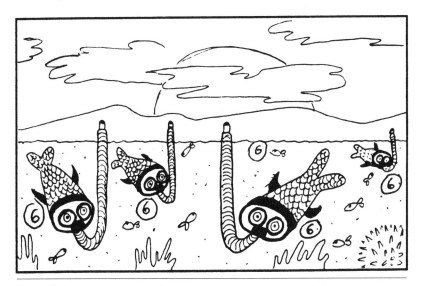

These Six-ish shad, smelt, sardines, and salmon are safely snorkeling.

They *hate* flattery!

Steve thought Shatzi loved him for his wonderful self.

Then he found out she just wanted him to feed her.

Six-ish children usually love what is true, good, and beautiful. They can be fearful of the unknown, they need to be in control, and they may tend to be pessimistic or paranoid.

You're all up to no good! Stop following me!

They like order and predictability
but can be changeable themselves . . .

Conducktor

and can go
from one
extreme to
the other.

They often have trouble making
up their minds.

After she thought of everything that could
possibly go wrong, Roberta made her decision.

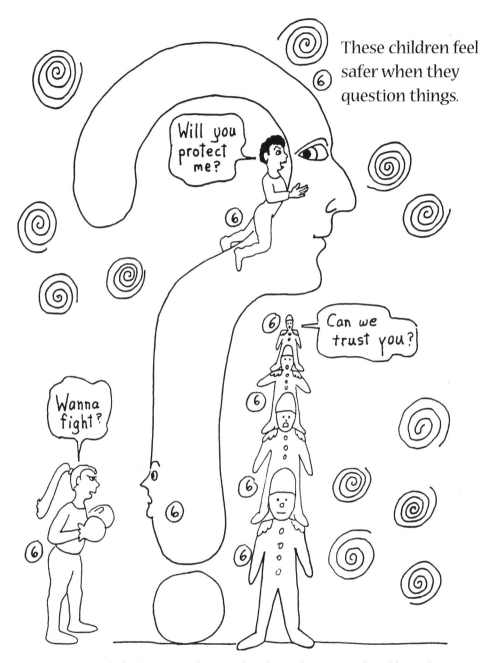

These children feel safer when they question things.

Questioner-style kids want to know who the authority is. They like to be out in front themselves but are usually nervous about it. Parents can help them learn to trust their inner authority by showing a quiet and steady confidence in their child's ability to meet new situations.

Approaching Ten Common Problems
with a Child in the Questioner Style

Questioners vary more than perhaps any other style and can be difficult to spot. They usually feel scared and suspicious inside, but some cover it up with a tough exterior.

Getting to School on Time

Most Six-ish children want to do things "right" in order to feel secure. Choosing what to wear or worrying that the mayonnaise in their lunch will spoil can make mornings a time of insecurity. Have them set their clothes out the night before, and make a peanut butter sandwich instead of using mayonnaise. When they're young, don't place too much of the responsibility for getting to school on them.

Study Habits

Many Questioner-style children love learning, want to do well in school, and try to please the teacher, who is a protective authority to them. Some (especially those with a strong Seven wing) expect their work to be "correct" the first time around and may not have patience for the groundwork: planning, research, and rough drafts. Ease the stress and anxiety of all children by teaching them to do their homework right after school and to start reports the day the assignment is given.

Manners

Fearful or phobic Six-ish children tend to be obedient and polite. Counterphobics may test or try to shock people; these antiauthoritarians will tease, poke, or make noises when the teacher's back is turned. Parents can help by taking a definite stand against negative behavior instead of laughing with embarrassment or ignoring sarcastic or rude remarks.

Getting Along with Others

Questioner-style children feel driven to control their environment, including other people. They may do it by being bossy or enraged or by being charming, ingratiating, and entertaining. Be steady, consistent, and dependable, and ask yourself if more structure in their life might help them to trust.

The rage exhibited by the Six-ish child may be frightening to others. Instead of overreacting or fighting against it, try to remain calm, and let your child's anger wind down by itself.

Winnie was introverted and loved to read books in hidden-away places. Her extroverted brother, Herman, would look for her, assuming she'd be delighted to have company; but she'd go into a rage and scare him off. He'd feel devastated. After he learned about personality types as an adult, he wanted to talk to her about their differences. She explained that she'd be lost in her reading and his surprise visits felt like invasions to her. She thanked him for trying to understand her. Their relationship improved rapidly.

Sleeping and Eating Habits

If anxiety attacks Six-ish children at bedtime or in the night, help them feel secure. Parents of Questioner-style kids advise not lying down in bed with the children while they fall asleep—their anxiety will likely start up again when you leave. Let them sleep with the light on, cuddle them, and/or talk their fears out with them. Encourage them to learn their own ways of adapting to stress and calming themselves down.

Six-ish kids sometimes develop anxieties about what they should or shouldn't eat. Have only healthful food around for snacks, and don't contribute to their concerns. Don't force or bribe them. Mealtimes can be difficult for many reasons, but try to maintain a calm and pleasant atmosphere for the good of your child and of the whole family. If children become disruptive, sit them up close to an adult. If necessary, send them to another room to eat.

Standing Up for Himself or Herself

Questioner-style children can often defend themselves from other people by means of their intellect or humor. Some scare people away by going into a blind rage. This isn't a satisfactory solution, so teach them ways to circumvent their temper. Since they worry about being overpowered, offer classes in the martial arts or in other sports that will help them feel physically competent. Counterphobic Six-ish kids will often engage in sports or build their bodies up on their own, while phobics are unsure of themselves, afraid of injury, and need extra encouragement.

Create opportunities for each of your children to be heard. This will help them feel comfortable about expressing their opinions outside of the home. Choose a teacher who does this, too, if possible.

Decision Making

Questioner-style children have trouble making choices because they want to have certainty about the outcome. This can be very slow and agonizing for all involved, and the resulting finality of the decision can feel terrifying to them.

When they get stuck worrying and trying to figure things out, they're unable to be very resourceful. They need reassurance to feel safe and calm enough to act.

Get-Up-and-Go

Six-ish children usually have a lot of energy, but they may be couch potatoes at times. If this is a problem, severely limit or put away the television and computer and offer choices of other activities. Questioner-style children typically react to the unknown with fear, negativity, or panic. Adults I interviewed appreciated having had parents who pushed them very gently into new situations, though they resisted at the time.

Responsibility

Six-ish children try to be conscientious and safe and are usually highly responsible. Taking responsibility says to a Six's parents that the child appreciates them and is also a way for kids to prove their trustworthiness. Help Six-ish children become their own authority by building up their self-esteem and confidence. Be supportive and reassuring but not overprotective. Try to remain stable in the midst of their unpredictability, mood swings, and testing.

Parents can make a big difference by gently exposing Questioner-style children to new situations. Gradually they build up confidence by seeing that the bulk of their fears and pessimistic predictions are unfounded.

Emotional Maturity

For Questioner-style kids, emotional maturity may come slowly, since their preoccupation with anxiety can hold them back. Introduce new things in small amounts to avoid surprises.

While others might be interacting with friends or learning new skills, Questioner-style children might be either trying to protect themselves or trying to prove they're tough and brave.

Notice what's going on when they're feeling secure and confident, and try to recreate these conditions. Trusting you is a rehearsal for trusting others and themselves, so avoid the appearance of hidden agendas. Be open and direct, and don't fuel Sixes' pessimistic imaginations. Answer questions to help them feel safe, and give them enough freedom to find their own ways of adapting to life's uncertainties. While it's often helpful to give children independence, this can cause anxiety and feel like a lack of love to some. Questioner-style children need structure and clear limits.

This Six-ish baby has a patient and understanding mother who's a Nine, the same type as one of his arrows. She supports him and tries not to scare him. Since her baby's quite nervous, she tries to pick calm playmates for him. When he's moody or changeable, she tries to stay balanced and centered within herself.

The Enneagram of Adolescence

The
Adventurer Style

Personality Quiz

Does your child

○ 1. wake up and fall asleep happy most of the time?

○ 2. seldom miss an opportunity to pocket a fascinating found object?

○ 3. like to be the star?

○ 4. like it when interesting people come to visit?

○ 5. have a sunny disposition and an infectious laugh or giggle?

○ 6. make lots of friends?

○ 7. have great curiosity and eagerness for knowledge?

○ 8. like to tell stories and jokes?

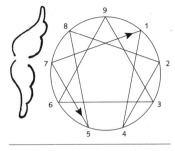

Wings and arrows

If most of your answers are yes, your child is currently behaving in the Adventurer style. This may or may not hold true in adulthood.

Whee! My Seven arrow helps me have fun!

In the head center,
Sixes show their fear,
Fives keep it to themselves,
and Sevens deny it.

If you haven't already, please read the Introduction before proceeding with this chapter.

Seven-ish children like to play . . .

and have fun with their friends.

They like to do many
  different things . . .

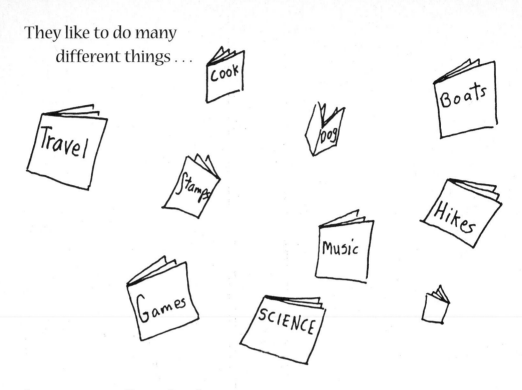

but sitting still in school
  isn't always one of them.
    They'd rather keep going
      and find new excitement.

They don't want to be restrained!

Adventurer-style kids try to charm adults into letting them do what they want. When they *really* want something, they don't give up.

I know I asked you if I could have a pet 100 times, but this time I REALLY mean it!

They're idealistic, love what the world has to offer,
and feel good about themselves.

The world is so plentiful!

A Seven-ish child has
a birthday party with
his arrows, the Five-
Observer and the
One-Perfectionist.

Words contributed by Maylie Scott

Seven-ish children feel supported and cheered on, and they give sparkling performances.

Seven-ish children's minds work overtime. Though adults may criticize them for not sticking with things, they can acquire considerable breadth of knowledge through experience and curiosity, they are often multitalented, and they can have high ideals. It's important to perceive and acknowledge their gifts and contributions, especially their appreciation of life.

Approaching Ten Common Problems with a Child in the Adventurer Style

Getting to School on Time

If Seven-ish children arrive at school late, they will try to wiggle out of the tardy list, usually successfully. Even though she got A's, Elaine was in trouble constantly for talking in the hall with her friends instead of getting to class on time. She folded the poor-behavior slips the teacher sent home in such a way that her father never knew what he was signing.

Study Habits

It's important for Seven-ish children to have teachers who keep things interesting and moving and who give individualized attention. Adventurer-style kids do best when they can pick and choose from a rich learning environment.

While this doesn't apply to all Seven-ish children, many have a short attention span. They tend to rush through one assignment to get on with the next, skipping details. Doing homework in two sittings would probably be more productive than trying to complete it in one. Some learn better by studying with a friend.

Adventurer-style children often become more serious and willing to buckle down in maturity. Their wings and arrows can influence their personality considerably. The Eight wing contributes decisiveness and strength, the Six wing concern about their future. Their One arrow contributes productivity and self-discipline, their Five arrow the ability to stay with one thing.

Many Seven-ish kids prefer to learn what's immediately applicable in classes that emphasize their talent at problem solving. They are very resourceful.

While consistency is very important in general with children, Adventurers need considerable flexibility from their parents and teachers, along with support.

My Seven friend, Happy, became more fidgety each time her father worked with her on reading. One day *she* had a brilliant idea, and he went along with it. They would take turns choosing unusual study sites—on the roof, in the tree house, under the piano, and so on. This gave her something to look forward to and stimulated her interest. Soon she felt more positive and relaxed about the process, and her reading improved immensely.

Ramy was curious. He liked to watch the water bags hit the ground. Sometimes they landed on people—"by accident."

Manners

Adventurer-style children charm their way through life and get away with manners that would get others in trouble. They like to tease, make fun of, and be the star. A Seven I interviewed said he liked to "torture insecure or vulnerable teachers." Seeing the teachers overreact to him made him feel powerful. Other Seven-ish children may annoy people by being impatient, trying to shock, or talking too much.

Teach Seven-ish children social skills, and encourage them to be direct and aboveboard. Make it clear that you don't like rudeness, but remain calm and centered.

Young Adventurer-style kids may be very active and pull things off store shelves. A busy place where many items catch their attention but activity needs to be held in check is not a good environment either for them or for your peace of mind. A restaurant that offers children's games or one that covers its tables with paper and provides crayons is better for both of you than a fancy restaurant.

Getting Along with Others

I feel like a grasshopper
in a world of ants.
NORRIS LYLE, A SEVEN

Though Adventurer-style children may be bossy or tease others, this is un-likely to be a major problem unless they have a strong Eight wing. Most Seven-ish children are free-spirited and good-natured; they get over upsets easily, they tend to skip over trouble, and they shun pain. They like fantasies, jokes, and keeping people entertained. Their stories bring people together.

Sleeping and Eating Habits

Seven-ish children don't like it when adults make them do things, but they do value a personal connection with you. They thrive on free-dom, but if you give them too much they feel ne-glected.

They're very active and get exhausted by the end of the day, but something fascinating can come along and charge them up again. Read or tell them quiet and calming (but not dull) bedtime stories.

My Seven-ish son didn't like to take much time out to eat, but some Adventurer-style kids love wonderful new eating experiences.

Standing Up for Himself or Herself

Seven-ish children will speak up for them-selves in order to avoid serious confronta-tions. They cleverly dodge fights (unless they have a strong Eight wing) by turning on charm, unexpect-edly telling a joke, or slipping away. If cornered, they may brazenly tell a lie.

Decision Making

If you come to a fork in the road, take it.
YOGI BERRA

Seven-ish children do not make decisions easily. They're often conflicted or ambivalent. They may say yes to a new idea, then feel horrified that now their options are narrowed. Or they may forget to think twice and commit themselves to doing something daring or confining, then ask in fear, "What have I gotten myself into?"

Get-Up-and-Go

Adventurer-style children are usually curious and motivated. They typically start each day full of plans, but they don't necessarily stick to them.

Summertime, about eight years old. Scooting along the great pavement of life.

George Woodward

Emotional Maturity

Since the style of Adventurers is to look confident and not reveal how much they may be hurting or anxious, it's important to show them consistent, tactful concern. Seven-ish children may not tell you about something upsetting because they're trying not to let it affect them, or they may be afraid of your reaction. Yet the upset did happen, and the hurt may fester and grow if it isn't resolved. The negative side of their optimism is that they may not develop the skills needed to cope with difficulties.

One Seven I interviewed said she hates to be left out—of groups, events, and discussions. This issue ran her life as a child. She would plan her own birthday parties to make sure she could do the fun things she wanted and that plenty of people and food would be there.

Some Seven-ish children lie to get their way, especially to authorities and especially if their parents are too strict. Rachel was so motivated to get out of the house at the age of thirteen that she passed herself off as being eighteen and got a job as a counselor in a summer camp. She also lied about being able to play the guitar, ride horses, and square-dance. Incidentally, she quickly learned how to do these things and was voted one of the best counselors at the camp.

Adventurer-style children may demand more freedom than they can handle. They often leave home at an early age and run the risk of staying young and immature. Rather than pointing out the negative things that might happen to them, help them find a positive direction. Support each new area of interest, and continually encourage them to be themselves. Trust that their exploring will eventually lead them to a place where things jell. Learn to appreciate their hunger for learning and for life, and let their adventurous spirit remind you to take yourself less seriously.

Responsibility

Seven-ish children are so busy that they may arrive late to activities. Sometimes they show up early, however, from eagerness to get started or to make sure thay avoid last-minute panic.

Most Adventurer-style children like doing jobs that are spontaneous. They get bored with daily routines such as washing dishes. Lackluster work is not appealing. With young Seven-ish children, as with all young children, give them work they can handle and take the most pride in. Add new responsibilities gradually until they're able to contribute to the daily running of the house. Rotating chores may help keep their interest.

Many Adventurer-style children are on a mission to better the world. They show responsibility by volunteering for causes—usually those they can work on with friends.

The Adventurer style is as legitimate as any other, yet it can threaten parents' sense of control, since they may not get the results they expect. Parents and teachers, falling into a Perfectionist style, may worry that if Seven-ish children aren't serious and work focused, they won't have the right life or a good life. But Seven-ish children feel especially judged by One-Perfectionist authorities. Seven-ish kids will blossom if you focus on their talents, if you gently guide and encourage them, and if you trust in their natural confidence.

The
Asserter Style

Personality Quiz

Eights show the most anger of the anger-center types (8, 9, and 1).

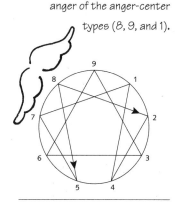

Does your child

    ○ 1.   rule other children?

    ○ 2.   have a great deal of energy and strength?

    ○ 3.   always make his or her presence known?

    ○ 4.   show anger and dissatisfaction freely?

    ○ 5.   give baby-sitters and teachers a hard time by being stubborn or bullheaded?

    ○ 6.   have a fast-running motor and need down time?

    ○ 7.   speak and act with authority?

    ○ 8.   behave exuberantly and enthusiastically?

Wings and arrows

If you answer yes to most of these, your child is currently behaving in the style of the Asserter. You can't tell whether an Eight-ish child will remain so in adulthood.

My Eight-ishness helps me out sometimes, but it can get out of control.

If you haven't already, please read the Introduction before proceeding with this chapter.

Eight-ish children can be fiercely protective.

They look out for their friends . . .

and defend those who can't defend themselves.

GO HOME!

These children take charge . . .

but what they want most of all is to feel connected to life's intensity. If their energy is not met through more and more fun and activity, heroic stories, or incredible experiences in nature, for instance, they may feel hurt and sad.

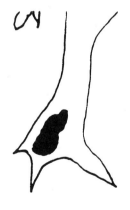

Miranda Copty

Asserter-style children don't hesitate
to tell people what they think of them.

Sometimes they seize control of their parents.

They work
hard and
play hard . . .

and hate
it when
people are
phony.

They can seek revenge and be intimidating, so people are often afraid not to go along with them. Raising Eight-ish children can be difficult because these kids can shift blame and not take responsibility for their behavior.

I'm SORRY, but I don't know how else to be!

On the other hand, people often misunderstand and blame them or judge them wrongly for their natural exuberance.

Tucked inside of Eight-ish children is their warm,
gentle, and vulnerable side. You will see it if you
earn their trust and respect. Be straightforward,
dependable, and honest with them.

Approaching Ten Common Problems
with a Child in the Asserter Style

Getting to School on Time

Some people . . . love to brag about jumping out of bed to watch
the sunrise and greet the new day and all that crud. I've never
actually seen a sunrise, but my guess is that it looks pretty much
like a sunset, except that it's on the other side of town.

D. L. STEWART, AN EIGHT

Unlike some children, who feel righteous about getting up early, Asserter-style children are more likely to feel grumpy about it. If they unleash their anger on you, try to keep your equilibrium and not react. Be firm about what needs to be done. Make mornings easier on yourself by doing some of the tasks the night before and/or putting on some music you like. Encourage your child to do the same.

Some Eight-ish children don't mind breaking a few rules. This can make training them to get to school on time difficult. See if you can make their school experience more attractive by enrolling them in extra activities (after-school clubs or ball games). Become involved in your children's classrooms to let them know you're interested and to keep track of whether their needs are being met.

Study Habits

Asserter-style children may have difficulty developing good study habits. Although they may protest loudly, these children need to learn to stick to homework routines. The best time is usually right after school. Parents need to be clear and consistent about what they and the teacher expect, and parents should check (or have someone else check) that Eight-ish kids' homework is finished before they can go out and play.

Manners

Manners don't usually come naturally to Eight-ish children, who are more likely to scowl, growl, and argue than to exchange pleasantries (this is especially true for Eight-ish boys). Poor manners can also be an effective way to shock

people or to take revenge. Having Eight-ish kids gives you the opportunity to see how realistic you can be. If you expect refined manners from them, you're probably not being realistic. Choose carefully which few manners are the most important and firmly enforce them.

Getting Along with Others

Asserter-style children usually have a sweet side and can be very thoughtful, loyal, and generous to their friends. However, many aren't flexible enough to get along well. They can be too sure of their own agenda and may impose harsh judgments on others. Many carry a chip on their shoulder and go ballistic if anyone laughs at them or touches their belongings. They tend to think of the world as a dangerous place where people aren't on their side.

Encourage Eight-ish kids to compromise, to learn how to read the moods of their playmates, and to recognize that when they have certain angry feelings it's time to count to ten and cool down.

Sleeping and Eating Habits

At the end of the day, read to Asserter-style children and develop some other bedtime rituals they enjoy. If they're still too energetic to sleep, let them wind down by themselves by playing quietly or reading.

Some Eight-ish kids are absolutely in love with food—with thinking about it, fixing it, and eating it. Make the most of this by inviting them to cook or bake with you. If your children are in the habit of eating from boredom—just to fill up the time—you may need to structure more things for them to do. If they misbehave at the dinner table, sit them up close to an adult (preferably) or send them to another room to eat. Never send children to bed without dinner.

Standing Up for Himself or Herself

Asserter-style children have a strong self-image and excel at putting themselves forward. Sometimes they overdo it. One mother said, "My Eight-ish son stands up for himself to the teeth in *every* circumstance, whether needed or not!" Remind Eight-ish kids, when they get the urge to fight, to evaluate the situation. Alternatives to fighting include compromising, walking away, or making a strong statement.

Eight-ish children are on the alert for injustices. When they become overly aggressive it is sometimes because they don't feel heard. They want to know that you're listening and engaged, even if you don't agree with them.

Catmospheric pressure

Decision Making

Asserter-style children usually have clear and definite ideas and almost never say, "I don't care" or "I don't know." It's important for parents to be firm and stay out of power struggles with them. Group decisions are a problem because Eight-ish children want to prevail. If your family has weekly meetings, cut off heated disagreements and put the issue on the agenda of the next meeting, when things will have cooled down.

Idea contributed by Ray Nelson

Get-Up-and-Go

The Asserter style is known for its ability to take action.

When Eight-ish children can't find anyone to match their energy and vigor, they're enormously disappointed. (Imagine how frustrated you'd feel if you had tons of strength and enthusiasm left for chasing and playing, but all of your playmates were tired and on their way home.) One Eight adult I interviewed said she overestimated her own power as a child and tried to stop a car that was rolling down the driveway by pushing on it. She was only five years old at the time.

Emotional Maturity

Eight-ish children are often immature when it comes to controlling their anger.

They can go nuts if they accidentally get bumped, for instance, or if something doesn't work right. They need firm, structured, and patient parents who can teach them how to get their minds on something else when they're angry. Time-outs don't help if the time is spent brooding over what has upset them. Keep your cool, for overreacting to their anger will prolong it. Be sensitive to the differences between you and your child. Instead of trying to whittle down Eight-ish children, focus on their virtues and strengths.

Responsibility

Asserter-style children are not usually sneaky and can be refreshingly honest. They can obey rules even when no one is supervising them. They're usually good at taking care of a younger child or pet or protecting a loved one.

Some tend to do best with routine chores like washing dishes; others prefer to do a task when it comes up, like bringing the groceries from the car to the house. Encourage young Eight-ish children to help by doing what they're good at. When they're older they can learn how to do other jobs that are useful.

My first child seemed Eight-ish, though he grew up to be a Nine. I tried to train him to put his blocks away when he was too young. I became Eight-ish myself (Eight is one of my arrows), and we'd have stand-offs where neither of us would budge. "Put them away." "I won't." "Put them away." "I won't." Finally, I realized this was ridiculous. You can't win contests with Eights over who can be more stubborn.

The Enneagram of Ecology

The
Peacemaker Style

Personality Quiz

Does your child

○ 1. like to watch TV, use the computer, or loll about the house?

○ 2. climb onto your lap to hug and resist getting off?

○ 3. inspire people to call him or her "sweet" or "accepting"?

○ 4. have trouble with decisions and go along with others most of the time?

○ 5. tell the family therapist everything is swell even when it isn't?

○ 6. move or speak a little more slowly than most other kids?

○ 7. get his or her feelings hurt fairly easily?

○ 8. have a stubborn streak?

If you answer yes to most of these questions, your child is currently behaving in the Nine style. This may or may not hold true as an adult.

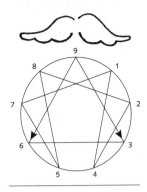

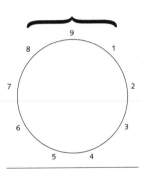

Wings and arrows

Anger or gut-center types feel connected to the physical world and make decisions according to what feels right in their body.

My mother was a Nine and very comfortable to be with.

If you haven't already, please read the Introduction before proceeding with this chapter.

Nine-ish children want everything to stay pleasant.

Clashes are very upsetting to them . . .

so they try to live harmoniously.

Miranda

These children can merge with others and take on the flavors of the other eight styles.

They're usually wise, goodhearted, and understanding.

Hey! You DO have a point!

While they usually have a mellow, relaxed personality, you can occasionally detect some anger in their voice or expression.

In fact, sometimes
they erupt!

Peacemakers are
often slow to
make up their
minds because
they see things
from many angles.

Nine-ish children often feel especially connected to nature. Others often see them as more easygoing than they feel. Treat Nines, as all children, gently. Show them you really see and hear them and value their presence.

Approaching Ten Common Problems
with a Child in the Peacemaker Style

Getting to School on Time

Nine-ish children have difficulty telling you directly what's wrong. If they can't get to school on time, make an effort to find out why. Are they getting enough sleep? Are they taking unexpressed anger out on you or the teacher? They may have inertia and may not want to stop doing what they're doing, whether in motion or at rest. It might help to play their favorite music while they're getting ready for school. Have a delicious breakfast ready for *after* they've done everything else. Remember, if you nag, these children become very stubborn.

Idea contributed by Michai Freeman

Study Habits

Some Peacemaker-style children get right down to business and study with enthusiasm. Encourage those who don't to do their homework at the same time every day, for Nine-ish children often get more done when they're in a habit.

Manners

Peacemaker-style children like to behave well to keep life pleasant and on an even keel. However, when they haven't expressed what they want (or don't know what they want), they may become stubborn or even aggressive. Help them feel confident and comfortable around others by providing a safe atmosphere within your family and by letting them know they're important.

Getting Along with Others

Nine-ish kids are not often social leaders, though they have great value as mediators. They often like to work behind the scenes. These children are biased toward seeing things positively.

Peacemaker-style children make generous and supportive friends and can be fun to play games and sports with. They're good companions on walks or long-distance runs, and they like sharing hobbies: collecting baseball cards, playing with dolls, or almost any other hobby you can think of. And they're known as the greatest to just hang out with. When they have problems with other children, it's more likely to be from overaccommodating than from aggression.

Sometimes they feel depressed, defeated, or discouraged because the harmony they seek is not easily achieved; however, they're resilient and get over it quickly.

Nine-ish kids may go along with authority figures for a long time then suddenly rebel or get stubborn.

Sleeping and Eating Habits

Nine-ish children enjoy sensual pleasures such as lying in the sun, sleeping, and eating.

If they seem stressed or unhappy, a good time to talk about it is while tucking them in bed. Give them plenty of time to tell you stories about their day.

Peacemaker-style children tend to be unhurried. Don't criticize or tease them if they're the last to leave the dinner table. Keeping things pleasant, which Nine-ish kids like to do, can itself create tension. For instance, Bertha would eat more than she really wanted of her mother's cooking because her mother would then be less irritable.

Standing Up for Himself or Herself

Peacemaker-style children tend to give in. Their powerful Eight-Asserter and One-Perfectionist wings can alter this considerably, though. Parents can help them with self-assertion by encouraging a change in their belief that they won't be liked if they put themselves forward. Create opportunities for Nine-ish kids to speak their minds, and set an example by speaking *yours* in a direct but nonthreatening way. Champion them, especially when they're young.

Get-Up-and-Go

Having too many possibilities can nearly paralyze Nine-ish children. When appropriate, help them clarify what they want. If they have clear goals, they'll go after them with great energy.

Decision Making

Sometimes Nine-Peacemakers are afraid people won't love them if they have needs, so they put off decisions and wait around to see what will happen. When they do make decisions, they usually consider their options deeply and seriously and don't shift their positions easily. To build their confidence, take an interest in their opinions, starting when they are very young.

Emotional Maturity

Many Nine-ish kids report that people say, "You're really sweet!" after they've known them only a short time.

Peacemaker-style children can be funny, comfortable to be around, and very warm. Be sensitive to how all styles of children react to you, and be aware of their moods—whether quiet, soft, upset, or anxious. If they're crying, gently try to find out why. If they're engrossed in building something, don't interrupt them. If they look unhappy, especially when very small, they *are* unhappy. Encourage them to snuggle up to you, and show them you enjoy watching them and listening to their feelings and ideas.

Nine-ish kids would love to have applause and approval for their accomplishments but are embarrassed when they get it. Don't let this stop you from showing your appreciation, though.

Responsibility

Peacemaker-style children usually want to do what's right and be responsible. A strong One-Perfectionist wing can reinforce this tendency. Sometimes they procrastinate, get sidetracked, or get stuck doing what they're doing.

Don't always protect Nine-ish kids. Experiencing the consequences of their actions will help teach them to be responsible for themselves.

Notice how your personality meshes with the Nine-ish child. Parents who are energetic and hard driving (Achievers or Asserters, for instance) don't always understand these contented, laid-back children. Six-Questioner parents can feel calmed by them. When Nine-ish children have strong Eight wings, they have a gentle strength that can be a source of security for the whole family.

After Carolyna grew up she continued to make peace a large part of her life. She has been teaching that creativity can prevent violence through developing the artist in everyone. Children and adults paint their visions of peace on tiles that are put together to make a wall. She acts as mother for these projects and teaches others to do the same. So far, she has made thirty-one peace walls in three countries.

Now that you've met all nine of the Enneagram styles, you may want to turn the page and play the guessing game.

The Guessing Game of Pets

☐

I'll make you happy!

"Caring Herring"

☐ ROAR!

Power Meeower

☐ "Right Whale"

WRONG!

NERD BIRD

☐ "Painted Lady" Butterfly

☐ Worker Bee

☐ Fun variety pack:

Pie-thon

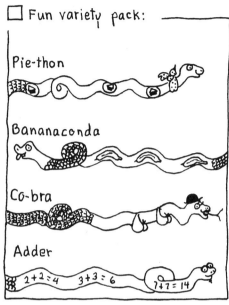

Bananaconda

Co-bra

Adder

2+2=4 3+3=6 7+7=14

☐ Peace Geese

☐ Nervous Newt

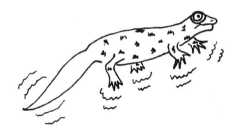

Parents
and the
Enneagram

The Nine Types as Parents

You may recognize yourself in these brief stories and descriptions.

One-Perfectionist Parents

Though firmness and structure can help children feel secure, some One parents could use more flexibility. Johnny's One mother had felt deprived of consistency in her own childhood. Since her work hours were irregular, she was afraid this might be upsetting her son in the same way. She stewed about it for a long time and finally got up the courage to talk to him about it. It relieved her to find out that he was more flexible than she and he *liked* having his days different from one another. Adults who were raised by a One parent often appreciated their parents' reliability but thought they were too critical.

Two-Helper Parents

Twos usually enjoy their children, like being parents, and encourage their children's interests. Because they're so involved, sometimes they do too much for their children instead of allowing the children to make mistakes and learn for themselves. Two-Helpers have trouble saying how they really feel or saying things that should be said but seem too negative, so they often manipulate their kids into doing what they want. Adults who were raised by a Two parent are divided between those who appreciated their attentiveness and involvement in their lives and those who felt smothered.

Three-Achiever Parents

A lot of parents, especially Threes, want their children to have Three-like qualities: energy, confidence, drive, and optimism. They think that if the children are cheerleaders, presidents of the class, and professionals they'll be successful and happy. But children come with their own personalities and can be successful in many different ways. It's helpful for Threes to look for and encourage the talents and interests in their children that are different from their own. Adults who are success oriented by nature appreciate what they learned from their Three parents. Others experienced their Three parents as too frenetic or pushy, and they complain their parents didn't spend enough time with them.

Four-Romantic Parents

While Fours have a lot to give in terms of insight, creativity, and warmth, they also need to support their children's interests, whatever they are. Fours can emotionally overwhelm children who are not at home in their world of feelings. Most kids won't be as sensitive as they are. Adults who were raised by Four parents often say they were charmed and fascinated by their parents or frightened of their emotionality and gloominess. Four parents often say they are overwhelmed by the beauty and wonder, and sometimes pathos, of having a child.

Five-Observer Parents

It's sometimes difficult for Fives to disengage from their own projects or thoughts and join in on the child's frequency. Five-Observer parents need to be careful, if their minds are on something else, not to become irritable or too authoritarian with their kids. Since Fives tend to compartmentalize, perhaps they'd feel comfortable setting aside a chunk of time each day for being truly present with their child. Adults who had Five parents sometimes say their parents' remoteness and negativity bothered them, but they enjoyed the Five's whimsical humor. Fives sometimes say their children interested them more as they grew into the teens and could discuss more complicated things.

Six-Questioner Parents

Six parents are very loyal, but they may be overprotective. It takes a lot of courage for Six parents to let their children out in the world where the dangers are, but kids are safer when they learn to solve their own problems. Six parents need to monitor their tendency to take the devil's advocate position, for this can erode children's confidence. The same is true with sarcasm and teasing. Adults who had phobic Six parents say the parents' constant fretting got on their nerves. Those who had counterphobic parents often thought their parents were too hard on them and expected too much. Both types of Sixes were said to have been devoted parents.

Seven-Adventurer Parents

Sevens like having playful children. But if the children are very serious, worried, or aggressive, Seven parents have to make big adjustments. Nancy, a Seven, took her Eight-ish baby on a trip to a foreign country, and he had a difficult time adapting to traveling around. She and her husband decided it would be best to spend the last half of the trip in one place. If being with small children feels restrictive, Seven parents might consider taking up some new interests that they can do safely at home and that can be interrupted. Adults who had Seven parents were sometimes confused by their parents' irregular hours at home but often enjoyed their stories and jokes. Some complain that their parents wanted too much attention for themselves or didn't listen to other people.

Eight-Asserter Parents

Eight parents are protective and can be good role models for taking action and having confidence. They need to be aware that anger can devastate children, and they need to try not to impose their will on them. Eights can have a difficult time adjusting to their children and perceiving how they are different from themselves. It is helpful to look for qualities in their children they may not be used to thinking of as strengths, such as the ability to back down or to show vulnerability. Adults who had

Eight parents react differently according to their type. Judy, a Seven daughter, was closely bound to her Eight father. He loved to show her off, play with her, and teach her songs as a young child. Later, he championed her singing and acting career.

Nine-Peacemakers Parents

Many Nines have a knack for being able to perceive and enter the world of a child. They can provide enormous warmth and understanding. Nine parents may need to work on following through with their children and being able to say no. Rather than always negotiating, they need to take a definite stand and uphold a position of authority. Adults who had Nine parents often say that they and their parents seemed merged. They say this felt secure, but making a separation was often problematic. Children of Nines appreciate their parents' flexibility in going along with and contributing to whatever interest they took up.

Parenting Philosophies

The following are statements written by actual people of each type. These are principles that these parents, psychologists, artists, scientists, and Enneagram teachers believe in and follow.

One-Perfectionists

*"What children need most is
affection and acceptance."*
AARON WACHTER

*"Be the best person you can be.
It's not what you demand or say;
it's how you lead by example."*
JOAN WAGELE

"Establish a value system and honor it consistently."
NAME WITHHELD
(this One was concerned that his statement might not be perfect)

Two-Helpers

"Don't try to protect your children by sugarcoating everything and masking real hurt. Be real and be honest about disappointment and unhappiness."
VICKI SILVA-SMITH

"Be a good role model by living your values and morals consistently. This can be applied to parents of children of any age."
SYLVIA FALCON

"Sense your children's sensitivities and individuality. We tend to think the children are just ours; they come from you but they aren't you."
VALENTINE ILLIDGE

Three-Achievers

"It isn't easy, but I make sure we have quality time. It's also important to express love, appreciation, and gratitude clearly and to make it safe to communicate anything, whether upsetting or joyous."
ALI MCKEON

"Unconditional love and support are essential. So is a willingness to realize that being a parent is a responsibility—a beautiful and satisfying one, but nonetheless a responsibility. These are easy things to say, but they're very hard to follow through on."
HANK SANCHEZ-RESNIK

"A parent's job is to support their children as they develop into unique individuals who can explore and express all dimensions of themselves. Parents do this by providing love, security, guidance, and a willingness to experience life with their children."
BELINDA GORE

Four-Romantics

"The most important thing is that the child feel perceived."
ANNEMARIE SUDERMANN

*"Don't interfere when children are testing their assertiveness
and working out their rightful place in the world."*
HOWARD MARGOLIS

*"When they are small children, acknowledge them for
having real feelings. Pay attention to them and make sure
they know they count. Kids are not just 'doing' machines."*
DAVID DEL TREDICI

Five-Observers

*"I want children to do what they enjoy doing. I try to make them
feel confident by not putting pressure on them. I don't have the
ability to make them do something they don't want to do."*
GUS WAGELE

*"When the parents work to make—and to keep—
their relationship honest and intimate, so their children
will see how healthy adults behave, and when the parents
offer their children the same honesty and intimacy, love
will naturally be there."*
GEORGE WOODWARD

*"I felt lucky that I had the tool of the Enneagram to use
when I became a parent. I didn't want to have the distance
with my son I felt with my father, who was also a Five, so
I went out of my way to be engaged and present from the
time he was born. I was also very protective, since he's a
Six-Questioner and seemed very sensitive and in need of it.
Being present for my outer child healed my own inner child."*
MICHAEL GARDNER

Six-Questioners

*"Spend enough time with the child to know
what he or she needs and wants."*
DAVID OLSON

*"Realize you can't teach, you can only be. Live as
a good example. My goal was to raise my son so he
could cope with a totally chaotic world."*
BOB FERNEKES

*"Combine freedom and structure in a way that enables them to
grow and at the same time feel safe. Give them a strong sense of
right and wrong. I've been the most successful at helping them to
be in touch with and express their feelings."*
ARLETTE SCHLITT-GERSON

Seven-Adventurers

*"Treat them as an important person and give them a
good self-image. Let them know—verbally and nonverbally—
that they're loved no matter what they do."*
NANCY KESSELRING

"Implant confidence."
MAYLIE SCOTT

*"As a teacher, I've seen too may parents impose
their own goals onto their children. Be there for
support no matter what, and let them be kids."*
CAROL OLSON

Eight-Asserters

"Get out of their way and don't mess them up."
JOYCE BURKES

"Find the joy in seeing and discovering the essence in each child."
PETER O'HANRAHAN

"It's imperative for both child and parents that the child be wanted. Beyond that, parents should present a lot of interesting possibilities and sponsor the child's mind and growth. The kids that are vital are listened to, read to, and taken places. Many kids these days aren't getting an interesting life; they're getting a second-hand, TV life."
MICHAEL COOKINHAM

Nine-Peacemakers

"Be aware of your child's inner experience."
BERTHA REILLY

"Teach them we're there for them. Keep them happy by giving them safety, security, and comfort."
HELEN MEYER

"Let them emerge instead of trying to shape them in your image. Trust and support them, and be aware that your worrying can be devastating to them."
GARY FOLTZ

"Love your children by being supportive and acting on behalf of their long-range welfare."
JIM WAGELE

Twenty Additional
Problem Areas

Most of the following subjects weren't covered in the previous chapters. Now that you've been introduced to the nine styles of children and learned something about adult Enneagram types, see how you can apply this knowledge to your family:

Bed-Wetting

Bed-wetting is considered normal for the first six or seven years. (Thinking we've failed as parents if our children aren't completely trained by two years old is also normal.) If your child is at least six years old, withhold *all* liquids after four or five o'clock and take the child to urinate before bed. Repeat this once in the night before you go to bed. Lead children all the way into the bathroom and onto or in front of the toilet, even if they refuse or insist they can't go. These children sleep very soundly. Sometimes they don't outgrow bed-wetting until twelve or fourteen or older, but this is rare. Be patient and don't scold, punish, or make them wash their own sheets.

Work out a system of rewards for over two or more days' success in a row, and keep it up for several months. Be supportive; this problem is difficult for the child, especially when it comes time for sleepovers or summer camp. Notice how your child reacts to bed-wetting: with guilt, fear, anger, nonchalance? Some kids are sure they'll stop wetting the bed tomorrow, while others fear they'll still be doing it when they're grandparents. Don't assume your child will respond the way you would or did.

Biting

If your small child bites you (or anyone else in your presence), be firm: "You *mustn't* do that! It *hurts!*" Try not to overreact. The child will eventually internalize your reactions and stop. Explain how the biting affects others rather than trying to convince the child he or she did a bad thing; this will be more effective and will help the child develop empathy.

Invite other children over only for short visits when your biter is relatively happy, rested, and well fed(!). Try to keep things calm, and choose more mature children for playmates, especially those who can defend themselves. Instead of focusing on your own anger or frustration, try to determine if there's a message in the biting. Is your child too tired? Is he or she trying to dominate the other? Does he or she want the other child to go away?

Clothes

Encourage your kids to choose their favorite colors, fabrics, and styles, within the limits of your budget. Even though this is difficult for parents who take pride in their sense of fashion, avoid imposing your taste on them. When appropriate, give children a push toward shopping for themselves.

Communication

When kids are tiny babies, talk to them a lot, in your language and in theirs, but don't talk baby talk to toddlers who are learning to speak. Listen to them without putting words in their mouths or finishing their sentences for them. Be forgiving if they say things they didn't really mean to say; try to remember a time in your childhood when you did this, too.

When it is appropriate to their age, set up weekly or biweekly family meetings. Pledge to listen with an open mind. Encourage open and honest expressions of feelings, and don't stifle contrary ones. Don't criticize or laugh at your children or try to squeeze feelings out of them they don't necessarily have.

When discussing a problem with your kids, think up as many solutions as you can together, then narrow the options down to one. Kids will try harder to make it work if they've been involved in the problem-solving process. Some families prefer to set up a meeting only when there's a pressing issue.

The golden rule ("Do unto others as you would have them do unto you") is not an ideal communication tool, because it assumes that we all want the same thing. It would be better to teach our children to empathize—to do unto others as *others* would like to be done to.

Suzanne and I were jabbering away as we drove to a gathering about an hour and a half away. Her ten-year-old son, Jules, sat quietly in the backseat. After twenty minutes, Jules sat up straight, leaned forward, and said firmly, " I think you should realize there are three people in the car and include me in the conversation."

We should teach our kids it's all right to speak up for themselves and to tell people what they need and how they'd like to be treated.

Indirect communication, such as through letters or art, is more comfortable at times. If your child has suffered a traumatic experience, drawing or painting the experience, dramatizing it, or telling the details to someone in a calm, safe environment can be healing.

Discipline

The more structure and predictability you have,
and the more you deal with your child in a kind
and firm way, the less you will have to punish.
STANLEY TURECKI, M.D.

Deliver a prompt and strong verbal message if your toddler starts to go in the street, play with electricity, or pull the cat's tail; then quickly remove the child from the situation. Set limits gently but with authority. With older children, you may want to write out some of the rules and the consequences for breaking them. If kids misbehave, use a serious and firm (not shrill or frightening) voice. Don't get into an argument about punishment. It's never necessary to discipline for discipline's sake, but if you need to punish, use a time-out or take away a privilege.

If children do something hurtful to another person, ask them to think about how the person might feel and how the situation should be handled.

Family routines can cut down on conflict and stress, but too much predictability feels like imprisonment to some free-spirited children. When kids are disciplined or criticized too much, they often show signs of feeling bad about themselves.

It's a common practice for parents and teachers to call a time-out when a child misbehaves and have the child go to his or her room or a quiet place for five or ten minutes. This removes the child from the scene of conflict, allows him or her to cool off emotionally, and interrupts negative behavior. It also gives the child the message that the behavior was unacceptable.

It's sometimes more effective to bring children closer to you—to give them your protection—instead of isolating them. They may be confused about the difficulty they've just had and may need to experience a positive attachment to a stronger adult ego. Bring them into the room with you to sit beside you or to be held. Let them express how they feel, and acknowledge their feelings. You might want to read the example of this in the "Siblings" section of this chapter.

Divorce

In children's minds, if one parent leaves, so could the other. It makes sense, then, that kids might regress to a former behavior—one that's familiar and makes them feel secure. Keep their lives structured and maintain the same discipline, keep celebrating special occasions like birthdays, and don't buy them a million toys. Also, be very careful about what you say about your ex-spouse, for they know that he or she is part of them. Explain the separation in such a way that they know it's not their fault.

Show your children you care about how the divorce affects them.

If you remarry, your children may not like it at all. Since you experience the relationship to your new spouse differently than your children do, explain that this is right for you, and reassure them that you still care very much about their feelings.

Drugs

Healthy attitudes about drugs and alcohol depend on your children's ability to trust themselves, make good judgments, and solve their own problems. Parental moralizing, controlling, and overprotecting are of no help. If children see their parents solve their own problems by numbing out with substances, the kids may do it, too. But even when parents are paradigms of right living, kids can still get into difficulty with drugs. Children who have confidence and are grounded in reality know when to stay away from a substance, when to stop experimenting, and when to walk away from a situation. Educate them about what narcotics can do to the body and mind. Tell them you're against drugs, yet let them know they're safe coming to you with problems. Children who feel accepted and competent and have interests and skills they enjoy are not as likely to become dangerously involved in harmful activities.

Parents usually feel guilty and angry when they learn their child is using drugs regularly. The child needs professional, parental, and family help, not punishment. Groups that educate and support parents can advise parents on how to confront the child and how to set up intervention and treatment, if necessary.

Some signs of drug use are behavior changes such as truancy, depression, hostility, poor grades, preoccupation, lying, and stealing. Physical symptoms include a dry cough, red eyes, and lethargy.

Resources include the National Council on Alcoholism and Drug Dependence (800-NCA-CALL) and Alateen (associated with Alcoholics Anonymous). Some schools and hospitals also have programs or make referrals.

Eating Disorders: Binge Eating, Overeating, Bulimia, and Anorexia

Eating disorders can be heartbreaking: parents can become so frightened and confused that they try to punish their child, both for the disorder and the secrecy that usually accompany these disorders.

Binge eaters and overeaters usually associate food and staying full with comfort and being loved. Anorexia (the inability to stop dieting) and bulimia (making oneself vomit) often start in puberty and occur more often in girls than in boys. Obsessive dieting and compulsive eating may be helped by going to Overeaters Anonymous. Sometimes other measures are needed.

Anorexics are at war with food and in love with the process of dieting. While anorexia accounts for more fatalities than any other psychiatric disease, it's difficult to convince anorexics that their urge to be thin is harmful. They usually need help from a caring professional program. In some cases, these children feel overcontrolled, overprotected, or excessively pushed to achieve. They often feel more powerful and in control of their dieting than of other parts of their lives. The physical dangers are great. Menstruation may cease in anorexics, and downy hair may grow on their bodies. Nutritionally, levels of zinc and other minerals can become dangerously low. Sociologically, we need to examine this culture's premium on thinness and its repulsion of heaviness. We also need to think about how often we discuss weight, especially in front of children.

When people habitually make themselves vomit, they have bulimia, the most common teenage eating problem. It usually begins as a way to control weight and then turns into an obsession. The acid from vomiting does a lot of harm, including eroding the enamel of the teeth. Bulimia is accompanied by guilt, secrecy, and personality changes. Both anorexia and bulimia can cause heart attacks.

It's important for people with eating disorders to stay in therapy or recovery, for often one addiction will replace another.

Call the information line of any major hospital for referral programs. Network through friends, the family physician, or your managed care program (HMO, health insurance) to find a competent therapist or recovery program.

Education

Create a stimulating environment in your home where dictionaries are browsed through, books are valued, and ideas and the arts are talked about. Be visible when you read, and read to your children a lot. Show them how to do crossword puzzles and other word games. Find out what they're interested in, and take them to the library to pick out books on these subjects. Learn to be computer literate to the point that you can find information about their interests on-line.

Take into account children's ages and different learning styles. Tiny babies like black-and-white or sharp-contrast things they can watch, such as mobiles; older infants perceive more subtleties in color as they develop. When kids can move around, provide a "nest" they can fool around in. Your holding and cuddling are much more important than are classes in raising a baby genius or teaching kids with flash cards. Notice your children's inborn learning styles, such as whether they respond more to what they see or to what they hear (multimedia programs and encyclopedias on CD-ROM appeal to both). Are they more self-referenced (Adventurers, for instance) or other-referenced (Achievers, for instance)? Do they like to start with an overview or with the details? Do they learn from analogies and stories, or do they prefer the straight facts? Do they take in information in a step-by-step or an impulsive way? Does competition stimulate them or make them nervous?

Teachers I've talked to are concerned that many children spend too much time away from home and are too tired to learn in the classroom. While many families have no alternative to childcare, perhaps parents could make a couple of changes in their schedules or take turns leaving one adult home with the kids while another does errands. These changes would enable the kids to be home a little more.

Friends

Show your children how to be tactful yet honest. Teach them how to introduce people to each other, how to handle disagreements, and how to word difficult messages diplomatically. Pairing your kids with others of different styles and temperaments can be balancing and stimulating.

Teach your children to be good sports. Instill in them the "sometimes you win, sometimes you lose" philosophy. If they're on a team, cheer them on to win *and* teach them to congratulate the other team when they lose.

Health

Don't underestimate how frightening a visit to the doctor can be. Choose a pediatrician who's sensitive to your children's feelings and takes time to explain what's going on. Some parents demand the impossible by telling children they're too big to cry over "a little thing" like a shot. Build trust by telling them the truth—that it will hurt but for a very short time. Let them know their fear is understandable, then gently divert their attention to something more pleasant.

Parents often spend too much time stewing about whether to call the doctor. This worrying itself can slow down a child's recovery. If at all in doubt about whether your child may be seriously ill, go ahead and call. The same goes for developmental questions, such as speech. If you have psychological questions about your child (such as a sudden change of behavior), yourself, or your family, make an appointment with a therapist.

Money

Managing money is an important life skill. Give young children a weekly allowance, not connected to chores, and open a passbook savings account for them. A One-Perfectionist-style child, especially, might enjoy keeping bank records and making sure they add up right. It's even more important that children who are not organized about such things start early to manage their money. Around the ages of twelve to fourteen, give them a monthly allowance for clothes.

For extra money, hire them to do jobs that you'd hire other people to do.

The Oedipal Stage

Around the ages of four to six, children become extremely attached to the parent of the opposite sex and leave the same-sex parent feeling rejected. When one of my daughters was this age, she assumed she would marry her father when she grew up. This phase is normal and necessary to children's growth and independence, but it also produces guilt and conflict. If all goes well, children realize (unconsciously) that they can't take the place of their rival parent. Whether you are the "rejected" one or the one they're "in love with," be understanding and tactful, but be firm about your loyalty to your partner. Try not to take it personally. Your steady attitude will contribute to a healthy outcome to this phase.

Parents with Differing Philosophies

Unless the marital relationship is protected and given a chance to flower and unless each individual in the partnership has his own chance for development, the family system becomes crooked, and the children become lopsided in their growth.
VIRGINIA SATIR

It's good to be honest in front of your children about most of your differences, as long as respect is shown. But try to come to agreements about rules in private, and present them to the children with a united front. Bargain with each other if it helps: "I'll agree to let her come home an hour later on weekends if you'll agree to go on more family outings." If a rule isn't working for one parent, renegotiate behind closed doors. If your parenting styles are very different (for example an organized, strict One and a laid-back, lenient Nine), try to have a sense of humor about it.

Sometimes one parent will take a certain stand just to be contrary to the other, a symptom of trouble in the relationship rather than real differences in philosophies. If your disagreements are causing undue stress for any member of the family, seek professional help.

When parents have different attitudes about learning, it's helpful to focus on a third element, the school. Rally around the teacher and what he or she is trying to accomplish. When parents don't agree about seeing a therapist, it's good for one to go alone.

Self-Discipline

When children are allowed to use their own resources and repeat what they're good at, they develop skills and self-discipline naturally. For example, my parents allowed me to spend as much time as I wanted picking out tunes on the piano. When I got bored with melodies, I figured out how to add chords. When I got tired of that, I added a bass line and ornaments, and so on. It wasn't always easy and I'd get frustrated, but I wanted to "possess" the music I had heard, so it was worth it to me to sit there working at it for a long time. I developed my ear this way. At the same time, I developed the ability to practice and study.

Adults often say that having an overcontrolling parent prevented them from developing self-discipline. Set up certain important boundaries and rules and enforce them. Otherwise, give your children the freedom to be themselves and to learn from the natural consequences of their behavior. Gus ate a large bowl of popcorn just before his mother served his favorite dinner, even though his father cautioned him against it. When his appetite returned, there was no tamale pie left. This incident contributed greatly to his self-discipline.

Teenagers will develop self-esteem, self-reliance, and self-discipline from having to come up with their own solutions to financial and other problems. Don't rush in and rescue them. Helping with a couple of honest mistakes is okay, however; everyone runs out of gas or gets stranded on a trip without enough money once or twice in life.

Sex

The subject of sex pops up now and then in subtle and unsubtle ways. Keep your sense of humor, and don't moralize. When your children are young, answer the questions they ask. Later, bring up the subjects you think are important (masturbation, menstruation, intercourse, birth control) in a caring way. Explain these things again at different stages of their development. Discuss AIDS and other diseases and the value of being mature in one's choice of a partner and in when to become sexually active. Give them pamphlets or books they can refer to on their own, and encourage them to come to you if they have questions or problems.

Some teenage girls have a baby in order to have something to love, to make a new life for themselves, or to receive the love and attention they don't feel they got as a

child. Those with vital interests and a strong sense of the future (a career or college) aren't likely to give them up to be pregnant. Teens are especially vulnerable to sex and drugs when they don't feel accepted by their peers. Even when they're very different from those around them, if their parents have shown them acceptance and love, they'll have confidence about who they are and what they will and will not do.

Siblings

The way to handle upset children's reaction to a newborn sibling is to encourage them to express their feelings and to acknowledge them. If your two-year-old slugs the baby, for example, pick the baby up to soothe him, and hold your two-year-old close while expressing your displeasure. Tell her she can't do that to the baby. Say, "I know you feel bad, but you can't hit." This is not rewarding the

behavior, but it's not telling the child she's a bad person, either. You have recognized her feelings as being valid. What she wants to know is that she's still important and special to you.

When friends or family come to visit your newborn, ask them to give the siblings equal attention. In case they bring a gift for the baby and not the older child, have some small presents on hand to give the child yourself.

Try to get the powerful emotion of envy out in the open where it can be handled. Almost all siblings fight and compete, but don't be too concerned as long as they also get along and the conflicts are not too extreme. Though it may difficult to do, because one child is always bigger or more aggressive than the others, try to let them work out their arguments on their own. Even when parents set an example of never ridiculing, belittling, or contradicting, children can often be cruel to one another. If one child shows an inordinate amount of fear, worry, accommodation, avoidance, or aggression toward another, consult a therapist.

Children whose personality styles resemble those of their parents often get more positive attention. The boldness of an Eight-Asserter-style kid, for example, may be appreciated by his Eight parent, while the quieter ones go unnoticed. Notice whether this happens in your family.

Single Parenthood

If you're a single parent, try to form connections between your children and other adults. It's good for children to be exposed to all types of people and to know that all grown-ups don't think and act alike. Also, they need to see their own style mirrored in others for validation. It's important that kids take an oppositional stance with their parent from time to time in order to mature and separate; if they're raised without much outside contact, the attachment to the parent may be so strong they won't risk having a disagreement. Encourage other relatives or friends to become involved in your children's lives so they won't need to depend only on you.

Some people choose single parenthood, and others find themselves suddenly in that role through divorce, death, or abandonment. Lu, a Seven-Adventurer, was a single woman in her late twenties considering becoming a nun. She was working in Africa at a mission station when a baby whose mother had died was brought to the hospital. They bonded. She decided to adopt him rather than enter the convent. Having had such a positive role model in her mother, a widow with six children, she found the decision to become a single parent relatively easy. Lu never regretted it. The baby brought her newness and excitement (especially when he reached the teenage years!), and she was still able to find fulfillment in other areas of her life.

Stress

How children experience stress is often related to their temperament. One may worry about being responsible for a pet, for example, while another with a comparable pet finds it no burden at all. Parents' personalities are another source of stress:

- "Stage mothers" (who may be either mothers or fathers), who live off the attention given to their children, can put tremendous pressure on children.

- Kids can feel denigrated if their One-Perfectionist parents are always on the alert for ways to improve them.

- Two-Helpers can intrude and belittle by giving too much advice.

- Six-Questioners may constantly caution and warn, which creates anxiety and gives children the message they can't take care of themselves.

- Envious parents can make life hard for kids who are prettier or stronger than they or who have exceptional abilities.

- Four-Romantics and Seven-Adventurers sometimes want to be told *they* are wonderful and can resent nurturing a child who begs for attention.

- Five-Observer parents can be too negative, indifferent, or authoritarian.

- Three-Achievers and Eight-Asserters can be too driving or too busy.

- When Nine-Peacemakers and other parents are too laissez-faire, children may experience the lack of guidance as stress.

Stress can be expressed in many ways, including unusual neatness, nail biting, excessive boasting, nervous tics, and so on. Try not to overreact to these behaviors. Don't underreact, either, and fail to look for a cause. If these symptoms are very upsetting to you or your child, consult a doctor.

Be aware of what impact your children's temperaments have on *you*. You may feel guilty if they have a sad outlook, if they are fearful, or if they are too negative or aggressive. Their constant talking, overintellectualizing, dramatics, or nervousness may rattle you. Even their virtues can stress you if you allow yourself to feel lazy, uptight, meek, incompetent, dull, or greedy by comparison.

Here are some references for finding help with *parental* stress:

Parents Anonymous, Inc., National Office, 675 West Foothill Blvd., Suite 220, Claremont, CA 91711. Phone (909) 621–6184. You might request their pamphlet, *Losing Your Kool with Your Kids?*

The Relaxation and Stress Reduction Workbook by M. Davis, E. R. Eshilman, and M. McKay. Oakland, CA: New Harbinger Publications, Inc., 1994

The Department of Social Services (check local listings)

The United Way (check local listings)

Teasing

Sometimes parents feel they're being funny or affectionate when they call their children names that refer to their physique, like "Shorty," "Tubby," or "Freckles." This behavior, as well as intense tickling, scaring, and shocking can feel diminishing to a child. If you think you've said something that could be taken as a put-down, apologize. If your kid doesn't laugh at something you think is funny, don't do it again. There are hundreds of ways to have fun with your kids that don't have negative effects on them.

Discover your children's gifts, feelings, interests, and needs, and gently expand their world to help them be more secure with who they are. This knowledge of your child will add much to your life, too, and will strengthen all family interactions. While conflicts are inevitable in a home, children should fundamentally feel connected, safe, comfortable, respected, and understood.

Adult Self-Portraits as Children

These drawings, by one adult of each type, are impressions of themselves as children. A few signed self-portraits can also be found within the chapters.

Afterword

Even though we adults usually relate to one type more than to the rest, we contain varying degrees of all nine types within us.

core type   wing   wing   arrow   arrow

shadow points

···

Recommended Reading

About the Enneagram

Baron, Renee (a Two), and Elizabeth Wagele (a Five). *The Enneagram Made Easy*. San Francisco: Harper-SanFrancisco, 1994. Original cartoons help get the points across. For Enneagram beginners or experts. Includes self-scoring inventories to find your type and a chapter on how the Enneagram and the Myers-Briggs Type Indicator system fit together.

————. *Are You My Type, Am I Yours?: Relationships Made Easy Through the Enneagram*. San Francisco: HarperSanFrancisco, 1995. Expands *The Enneagram Made Easy* but also stands alone. Written in the same style, it includes subtypes, famous people, how each type gets along with each other type, lookalikes, and how the Enneagram and the MBTI work together to explain relationships. The humor helps couples relax when talking about their relationship.

Condon, Thomas (a Six). *The Enneagram Video and Movie Guide*. Portland, OR: The Changeworks, 1994. I refer to this book all the time. A good way to pick movies and learn types and type interactions.

Horney, Karen (probably a Five). *Our Inner Conflicts*. New York: W. W. Norton, 1945. While not specifically about the Enneagram, chapters 3, 4, and 5 are relevant to the centers. Based on keen, concrete observations.

Hurley, Kathleen V. (a Three), and Theodore Dobson (a Four). *What's My Type?* San Francisco: Harper-SanFrancisco, 1993. Creative and healing insights into the Enneagram.

Naranjo, Claudio (a Five). *Character and Neurosis*. Nevada City, CA: Gateways, 1994. Naranjo contributed much of the psychospiritual development of the Enneagram. Extremely insightful. For advanced students.

Palmer, Helen (a Six). *The Enneagram*. San Francisco: Harper & Row, 1988. This comprehensive study and her *The Enneagram in Love & Work* (HarperSanFrancisco, 1995) are standard books on the Enneagram. She is known for classes in which she interviews exemplars of the nine types.

Riso, Don (a Four). *Personality Types*. Boston: Houghton-Mifflin, 1987, updated in 1996. Another Enneagram standard by prolific Riso. Also *Understanding the Enneagram*. Boston: Houghton-Mifflin, 1990. I also recommend the books by Riso and his collaborator, Russ Hudson (a Five).

Rohr, Richard (a One), and Andreas Ebert. *Discovering the Enneagram*. New York: Crossroad, 1990. Approaching the Enneagram from the point of view of spiritual direction. Powerful writing and a gentle sense of humor. Rohr is a respected Franciscan writer; Ebert is a Lutheran minister.

Thomson, Clarence. *Parables and the Enneagram*. New York: Crossroad, 1996.

Enneagram Periodicals and Resources

The Changeworks Catalogue, P.O. Box 10616, Portland, OR 97210–0616. Tapes and books by Thomas Condon and others on the Enneagram, NLP, and Ericksonian Hypnosis.

The Enneagram Educator. Its editor, Clarence Thomson (a Seven), is a creative writer and thinker. This lively publication comes out four times a year. You can order books and tapes from it and find out what's new. Available from *Creedence Cassettes Catalogue,* 1–800–333–7373.

Enneagram Monthly, 117 Sweetmilk Creek Road, Troy, NY 12180–9510. Articles on the Enneagram from many viewpoints.

The International Enneagram Association's Newsletter, P.O. 2625, Westfield, NJ 07090–9998.

On Parenting

Brazelton, T. Berry. *Touchpoints: Your Child's Emotional and Behavioral Development*. Reading, MA: Addison-Wesley, 1992. Relaxed style. Makes you feel good. Loaded with well thought out information based on years of experience.

Brooks, Andree Relion. *Children of Fast-Track Parents: Raising Self-Sufficient and Confident Children in an Achievement-Oriented World*. New York: Penguin Books, 1989. How different kinds of children react to hard-driving parents.

Caron, Ann F. *Don't Stop Loving Me*. New York: H. Holt, 1991. A guide for mothers of adolescent daughters.

————. *Strong Mothers Strong Sons*. New York: HarperPerennial, 1995. Very thought provoking, written with frankness and a sense of humor. Great for parents of preteen and teenage boys.

Eisenberg, Arlene, Heidi E. Muroff, and Sandee E. Hathaway. *What to Expect: The Toddler Years*. New York: Workman Publishing, 1994. Very complete and well written. Other good books in this series, too.

Elium, Jeanne, and Don Elium. *Raising a Son*. Berkeley, CA: Beyond Words Publications, 1992. This book and the Eliums' *Raising a Daughter* (Beyond Words, 1994) cover children all the way up to age twenty-nine.

Eyre, Richard, and Linda Eyre. *Teaching Your Children Values*. New York: Simon & Schuster, 1991. Influential writers discuss social values.

Faber, Adele, and Elaine Mazlish, *How to Talk So Kids Will Listen and Listen So Kids Will Talk*. New York: Avon Books, 1982. Based on the work of Dr. Haim Ginott. Chapters include "Helping Children Deal with Their Feelings" and "Freeing Children from Playing Roles." Good ways and bad ways to parent. Exercises and stories.

Fraiberg, Selma H. *The Magic Years: Understanding and Handling the Problems of Early Childhood*. New York: Charles Scribner's Sons, 1959. Takes us into the child's mind and analyzes how imagination operates. Also explains how children acquire morality and learn to control their impulses. Treats subjects such as anxiety, fear, eating disturbances, toilet training, biting, language, ego, conscience, the oedipal stage, and guilt.

Gold, Mark S., M.D. *The Facts About Drugs and Alcohol*. New York: Bantam Books, 1988. An amazing amount of information. Chapter 2 is titled "The Facts About Adolescent Drug Abuse."

Lighter, Dawn. *Gentle Discipline: 50 Effective Techniques for Teaching Your Children Good Behavior*. Deephaven, MD: Meadowbrook Press, 1995. Short, clear, no nonsense. For parents of children from birth to age nineteen.

Napier, A., and Carl Whitaker. *The Family Crucible*. New York: Harper & Row, 1978. If you have doubts about what family therapy can accomplish, read this.

Nelsen, Jane, and Lynn Lott. *Positive Discipline for Teenagers: Resolving Conflict with Your Teenage Son or Daughter*. Rocklin, CA: Prima Publishing, 1994. This will be useful to you and your family during these years.

Pantley, Elizabeth. *Kid Cooperation: How to Stop Yelling, Nagging, and Pleading and Get Kids to Cooperate*. Oakland, CA: New Harbinger Publications, 1996. Full of tools to use along the path of parenting. The story on page 80, alone, is worth the price of the book.

Pipher, Mary. *Reviving Ophelia: Saving the Selves of Adolescent Girls*. New York: Ballentine, 1994. Contains dozens of personal stories—a view of how our culture influences children.

Seligman, Martin E. P., Ph.D. *The Optimistic Child*. Boston: Houghton Mifflin, 1995. Practical ways to build optimism and self-confidence.

Turecki, Stanley I., M.D. *Normal Children Have Problems, Too*. New York: Bantam Books, 1995. For parents of children from three to twelve. "The essence of my approach is to look at problems and devise solutions for *the individual child and family.*" If you tend to feel guilty, you'll find this soothing.

———. *The Difficult Child*. New York: Bantam Books, 1989. Emphasizes children's innate makeup or temperament. A very practical, reassuring, and wise book.

On How to Be a Good Parent, for Readers Twelve Years Old and Up:

Ackerman, Albert, *The Buddha's Treasure,* 1996. Write to Dr. Ackerman, 8 Captain Drive #451, Emeryville, CA 94608, if unavailable in your bookstore. A novel about a thirteen-year-old Five-Observer whose sarcastic Eight-Asserter father constantly criticizes him. They go to China in search of an exotic medicine and return with unexpected results. My favorite quote is "Parents raise children. They must also allow their children to raise them."

Thanks for your help:

Gus Wagele, Maylie Scott, Peter O'Hanrahan, Tom Clark,
Penny De Wind, Harry Gans, Cathy Valdez, Gail Wread

Albert Ackerman, Jan Ayres, Sharon Berbower, Bayla Bower, David and Judy Burke, Joyce Burkes, Elaine Chernoff, Michael Cookinham, Miranda and Ramy Copty, Mary Beth Crenna, Madonna Datzman, David Del Tredici, Helen Del Tredici, Sylvia Falcon, Bob Fernekes, Fran and Gary Foltz, David Freeman, Michai Freeman, Michael Gardner, Nick Gerson, Belinda Gore, Frieda Hedges, Richard Hendrickson, Valentine Illidge, Fred Isaac, Nancy Kesselring, Steve Kruszynski, Rita Largman, Harriet Whitman Lee, Norris Lyle, Howard Margolis, Carolyna Marks, Rebecca Mayeno, Lin McGuigan, Ali McKeon, Helen Meyer, Ed Mooney, Trevor Nelson, Carol and David Olson, Louise Paré, Elizabeth Ratcliff, Bertha Reilly, Hank and Lucienne Sanchez-Resnik, Maria Saxton, Arlette Schlitt-Gerson, Grace Shireson, Vicki Silva-Smith, Annemarie Sudermann, Suzie Torrano, Bob Valdez, Aaron Wachter, Augie Wagele, Jim and Joan Wagele, Martha Wagele, Nick Wagele, Elin Weiss, and Ann and George Woodward.

Also to Linda Allen, my agent, and to John Loudon, Karen Levine, Mimi Kusch, Ralph Fowler, and others at HarperSanFranciso.

I wish to thank everyone who contributed the initialed or signed self-portraits within the chapters and on the "Self-Portrait" page and those who contributed to the "parenting philosophies" pages.

··

About the Author

Elizabeth Wagele is a writer, musician, and
professional cartoonist. She is the coauthor of
The Enneagram Made Easy: Discover the 9 Types of People and
Are You My Type, Am I Yours?: Relationships Made Easy Through the Enneagram.

Please visit her website at: http://www.slaydesign.com/enneagram/.